FOREWORD TO CENTENARY EDITION

"The Little Red Town and JMB"

On 27th December 1904 the theatre-goers of London were set back on their heels by a production of ground-breaking imaginativeness.

Yes, it <u>was</u> the first performance of James Matthew Barrie's "Peter Pan".

The man whose roots were dug deep in the little red town of Kirriemuir (the motto of which, "Jamais Arriere", means "never behind") had created an innovative theatrical masterpiece, incorporating some of the wizardry of the magician and the trapeze artist.

By so doing, he opened up a whole new world of possibilities for 20th century theatre.

Since then, the story itself has enjoyed myriad incarnations.

It has been printed in versions abridged and unabridged as a novel for children, and for adults.

Translated into most of the world's languages, it is recommended reading for children from Japan to the USA.

Some of the world's foremost artists and illustrators have been stimulated into creating visual images equal to the magic of the original fantasy.

According to www.peterpanfan.com, as a musical it was given 3 Tony Awards in 1955. Most recently, America's Cathy Rigby reprised her starring role in it to critical acclaim which identified her as "arguably the best Peter Pan ever to hit the stage".

A few years ago, this show took Australia by storm as well.

In addition, it has been set as a play, a children's musical, a pantomime and a ballet.

Film versions abound. It was made into a silent film in 1924 and a Walt Disney cartoon, costing 4 million dollars, in 1953. Its more sinister aspects were edited out for this version, and for most youngsters, even today, this adaptation is unfortunately thought to be the original of the tale. It is now mostly watched as a video or DVD at home.

In 1991, Steven Spielberg moved the story forward in time with his film, "Hook", for Universal Pictures.

Stars of the magnitude of Dustin Hoffman, Robin Williams, Julia Roberts and Bob Hoskins saw fit to accept major parts in it.

Disney gave his original cartoon a make-over into "Return to Neverland" in 2002. In it, Wendy had a daughter who seemed less enamoured with PP than her mother! Like "Hook", it was a major cinema success.

To mark the centenary of the first performance, two multi-million movies were made.

In 2003, Mohammed Al Fayed was a principal investor in P.J. Hogan's state-of-the-art animated film, unmistakably entitled "Peter Pan". He saw it as a most appropriate memorial to his son, Dodi, killed alongside that fairytale princess, Diana, Princess of Wales.

For the makers of this film, close adherence to the original plot was a must. This was one of the few occasions when Peter Pan was played by a boy (Jeremy Sumpter).

In November of 2004, Miramax hit the big screen with "Finding Neverland". Involving three different film studios and focussing on Barrie himself, it had its Scottish premiere at the Odeon at Douglasfield in Dundee. I had the privilege of highlighting Barrie's Kirriemuir roots on that occasion.

Whilst taking liberties with a few facts and the chronology of events in Barrie's life, it painted a sympathetic picture of him and his compassion for human suffering, especially that of the Llewelyn Davies family.

Oh, how JMB would have loved to be as 'tall, dark and handsome' as Johnny Depp!

Dustin Hoffman portrayed Charles Frohman, the impresario who had the courage to keep faith with genius, despite occasional setbacks. Kate Winslet was a beautiful, delicate yet strong-willed Sylvia Llewelyn Davies, and Radha Mitchell played that rather overlooked person in Barrie's life, his wife, Mary Ansell.

Freddie Highmore received an Oscar as Best Newcomer for his interpretation of Peter Llewelyn Davies, who was to protest to his dying day that it was not he, but Barrie, who *was* Peter Pan.

The combination of Barrie's inescapable Scottishness in this film and the centenary itself has produced unprecedented media interest in the impact of Kirriemuir on him.

What better time, then, to re-print this little volume which aimed to outline the heritage of his Kirriemuir and detail for posterity the strength of its place in his heart?

So how has life been in "the little red town" since we first told its story?

Outstandingly, technology has become a dominant part of society worldwide.

In the late 1970's, George Sampson (see "Dedication") recorded in his log that "there is as yet no evidence of the micro-chip in Kirriemuir".

Ah well, it arrived not long afterwards, and nowadays Kirriemuir is up there with the best of them! This second edition itself is testimony to such progress, being re-produced by scanning and digital "print-on-demand" techniques.

Kirriemuir as a community of some 7000 folk has been moving forward too, with lots of new quality housing and all the schools being upgraded to meet 21st century demands.

In common with much of the UK, changes in shopping trends have threatened the viability of local shops, but, with dogged determination and entrepreneurial use of the Internet, most of them have 'hung on in there'.

J & D Wilkie Ltd. remain the main employer, maintaining production of a variety of synthetics, among them camouflage material and other industrial textiles.

The Strathmore Valley is as fertile as ever, but some kind of agricultural revolution has seen barley, beef and berries diminish, and methods of production and harvesting radically change. Gone are the days of holidays spent picking tatties or berries, and in to our native place have come new giants – harvesters of peas, potatoes, berries, oil seed rape and other grain. Great swathes of regimented polythene Nissen huts help propagate the berries, mostly furth of Kirriemuir itself, while metallic ones shelter piglets.

The main tourist attractions have continued to welcome visitors in pleasing numbers. A partnership between the National Trust for Scotland and Angus Council has enabled the Camera Obscura to be modernised and open to the public throughout the same season as Barrie's Birthplace, April till September.

Richard Moss's private Aviation Museum brings enthusiasts from around the world. The Den is still the only place in which to roll your Easter Egg satisfactorily and Visocchi's ice-cream draws the crowds in their drouthy droves as it has done since 1930!

It is worth recording that, for several years, the Peter Pan Gateway Trust worked very hard to try to have a 21st century visitor attraction created on the 7 acres of Pathhead Farm so generously donated by the now deceased Allan Bruce.

This was to have marked for all time the fact that Kirriemuir and its Glens were the main wellspring from which so much of the life's work of Sir James Matthew Barrie, Bart, OM, was drawn, not least "Peter Pan."

Our vision was for an eco-friendly, natural, weather-proof children's paradise, "not large and sprawly, with tedious distances between one adventure and another, but nicely crammed" (J. M. Barrie: *Peter and Wendy*). Ideally, it would have opened its doors in the centenary year of 2004.

Sadly, it was not to be: we could find no Frohman. We did make sure, however, that every child who was a pupil in the town or rural primary schools at the Millennium experienced the story of "Peter Pan" through the Purves Puppet Theatre's version.

The good news is that there has been a pleasing upsurge of interest in the social, economic and cultural history of Kirriemuir and the Glens. A great deal of research, an exhibition and several publications were spawned by the Millennium. Others have followed.

Kirriemuir's principal Millennium project took the form of an amazing sculpture in red sandstone by Bruce Walker. Entitled "The Circle of Time", it consists of a huge globe of the world over which water from a nearby ancient artesian well cascades. It represents the philosophical belief that time is a continuum, a circle without beginning or end.

The Quatercentenary in 2004 of the Town House, extensively renovated at the turn of the century to house our now award-winning Kirriemuir Gateway to the Glens Museum, was combined with the Peter Pan Centenary to stimulate a summer of celebrations.

400 years of heritage were evoked in two dramatic performances loosely based on events and characters from Kirriemuir's colourful past: "Cronies 'n' Closies", street theatre which took people through some of the nooks and crannies of the old town, and "Common Threids", a drama staged in and around the Glens and Kirriemuir Old Parish Church.

I conducted some guided walks "In the Footsteps of JMB" and two lectures were given about Barrie: on 25th June, Dr Karen McGavock, Kirrie born and bred, shared her impressive knowledge of Barrie's life and work; and on 1st December, Professor Ronnie Jack, recently retired from the Chair of Scottish and Medieval

Literature at Edinburgh University, left his audience in no doubt that the man was indeed a genius, in many ways ahead of his time.

Barrie's gift of his copyright and other intellectual property rights of "Peter Pan" to Great Ormond Street Hospital in 1929 has generated undisclosed millions of pounds for the hospital, and truly helped to make it "great". A special dispensation by Parliament has allowed this beneficence to continue without limit of time in the UK.

Even now, the hospital has commissioned Geraldine McCaughrean, one of Britain's most prolific and talented writers for children today, to write a sequel.

Ms McCaughrean is quoted on www.gosh.org as saying "It is an astonishing, daunting privilege to be let loose on Neverland, armed with nothing but a pen, and knowing that I'm walking in Barrie's revered footsteps....but completing this book is going to be the writing adventure of a lifetime." Her provisional title is "Captain Pan".

Barrie's great- great-nephew, David Barrie, Chief Executive of the National Art Collections Fund, was one of the judges of the competition to choose the author.

"Captain Pan had a real fight on his hands, but he won through in the end. I think J M Barrie would have liked his style – if I'm wrong, he'll be back to haunt us!"

So there you have it.

One small town.
One small man.
One magnum opus.

Sandra Affleck, June 2005.

v

ABOUT THE AUTHOR

Sandra Affleck came to Kirriemuir when her husband became a Headteacher there in 1973. In the late 1970's, she began researching the history of the town and its famous author.

Her first book was "A Guide to Kirriemuir and District" which was published by James Norrie Ltd in 1981. Subsequently, she gave illustrated talks and guided walks, and contributed to several leaflets aimed to inform visitors to the town.

In 1985 she was a key player in "Anniversary Celebrations Eighty-Five" which marked both the Centenary of the Town Hall and the 125th anniversary of Barrie's birth.

Affleck Publications first produced "The Little Red Town and JMB" in 1990, and in 1996, they published, on its centenary, a re-print of the first-ever Guide Book to Kirriemuir, "Through Thrums."

2004 saw Sandra compile the text for the Quatercentenary Calendar of the Town House, and, with Helen Main, research and write the story of the 20th century in the Southmuir for the Centenary of St Andrew's Church. "Views of the Southmuir" includes the story of the happenings in Barrie's second Kirriemuir home, "Strath View".

In 2005 she appeared on BBC2's "Castle in the Country" series, speaking about Barrie's Kirriemuir roots.

The
Little
Red
Town
and JMB

by

Sandra
Affleck

Authors On Line

Visit us online at www.authorsonline.co.uk

2

The Little Red Town
and JMB

The Lifestory of Kirriemuir
and its place in the life of
Sir James Matthew Barrie, Bart.

by Sandra Affleck

Kirriemuir 1990

3

"She told me everything,
and so my memories
of our little red town
are coloured by her memories."

James Matthew Barrie
in "Margaret Ogilvy"
1896.

THE LITTLE RED TOWN
and JMB.

CONTENTS

PART TWO: THE J.M.B. CONNECTION

DEDICATION

In all sincerity, this book is dedicated to the memory of Mr. George Sampson who, from the early 1920's to the late 1960's was a solicitor's clerk with the firm of Wilkie and Dundas, Marywell Brae, Kirriemuir,

As a result of a chance remark made to him in 1922, shortly after his arrival in the town, by a former Headmaster of Reform Street School, he began taking notes of historical facts from the title deeds of the many properties which passed through his hands, "in case any future historian may find them helpful."

In 1968, he had the notes typed out and sent to the Scottish Records Office in Edinburgh. They made three bound copies, retaining one in their Topographical Section, and sending the others back to Mr. Sampson.

These notes were entitled "From Hamlet to Town".

When I was researching for my "Guide to Kirriemuir and District" which was first published in 1981, he generously made his own copy, which he was even then in his retirement up-dating, available to me.

Following his death in 1984, his widow most graciously entrusted it, and all his other books and research material, to me, on the understanding that it would eventually find its way into the Kirriemuir Public Library.

Most, therefore, of all I have learned about the buildings and streets of Kirriemuir, particularly in their earliest days, has derived from his meticulous research.

I am only sorry that he did not live to see either how we celebrated the heritage of Kirriemuir in "Anniversary Celebrations Eighty-five", or this long-time-coming book of mine.

I can only hope that it does justice to his work.

Sandra Affleck
Kirriemuir
1990.

8

INTRODUCTION

"The Little Red Town" of Kirriemuir lies a little way off the beaten track, just a few miles from historic Glamis Castle, in the heartland of rural Angus, pride of Scotland's fertile plain of Strathmore.

Long described as "the gateway to the glens", it is also only some fifteen miles from the North Sea, and more or less equidistant between Edinburgh and Aberdeen.

To the south, cut off from sight by the rolling line of the Sidlaw Hills, are the silvery Firth of Tay and "The City of Discovery", Dundee.

To the north, the skyline is dominated by the foothills of the Cairngorms, where the glen roads lead towards Royal Deeside.

All around is abundant evidence of ice-age land formation, that in itself a process of nature first recognised by a son of Kirriemuir, the eminent geologist, Sir Charles Lyell of Kinnordy. Archaeologists too have found remains from the Bronze Age, and Pictish, Roman and Celtic cultures.

But, despite such antiquity and natural beauty, Kirriemuir was a town of which few people had heard until one James Matthew Barrie became famous as a playwright, especially of "Peter Pan", and it emerged that he was a native of the place.

Inspired by his mother's memories of it, he wrote much, in his apprentice years, about Kirriemuir in its heyday as a centre of hand-loom weaving. But by the time he was nine, the Industrial Revolution had penetrated even "Thrums", and a whole new world was beginning. The erstwhile hamlet, or couthy "ferm toun", was set to become a thriving, lively and industrious town, and to remain so until well into the twentieth century.

I have two aims, therefore, in this book.

One, to put together a reasonably coherent record of the lifestory of Kirriemuir, the heritage among which native and incomer alike live today, and which is fast disappearing in a whirlwind of change; and two, for the very first time, I believe, to chronicle in detail Barrie's connections with, and visits to, the town of his birth, so that people may better judge for themselves how much his "Kirrie connection" meant to him.

I must emphasise that this volume contains my personal understanding and individual interpretation of events, based on as detailed and accurate research as I have been able to undertake. Nevertheless, it cannot, and does not claim to, be without omissions or errors.

Hopefully, "warts and all", it will go some way towards bridging the gap between yesterday and tomorrow.

Sandra Affleck.
1989.

The Little Red Town
and JMB

Part One
From Hamlet to Town

CHAPTER ONE

THE DAYS OF THE HAMLET

Kirrie or Killie?

To begin with, something of a riddle!

How did Kirriemuir get its name?

Should it in fact be "Killiemuir"?

More than thirty different spellings - and therefore presumably pronunciations - of the name have been recorded as in use during the ages before the standardisation of spelling.

These include: Kerymore, Kerremuir, Killemure, Kylymure, Killemuir, Killemoore, Kirrimoore. One legal document dated 1694 contains within it both "Killimure" and "Kirriemuire" - very confusing!

The choice of prefix appears to be between "Ker" and "Kil", and of suffix, between "Mor" and "Muir". To turn to Gaelic for further enlightenment seems logical.

"Carrou (Gaelic spelling 'ceathramh') Mor" means "the big quarter", and it is thought to refer to the 12th century Sherriffdom of Angus, of which "The Quarter of Kerymure" was physically the biggest. There is something slightly chicken-and-egg about this theory, however.

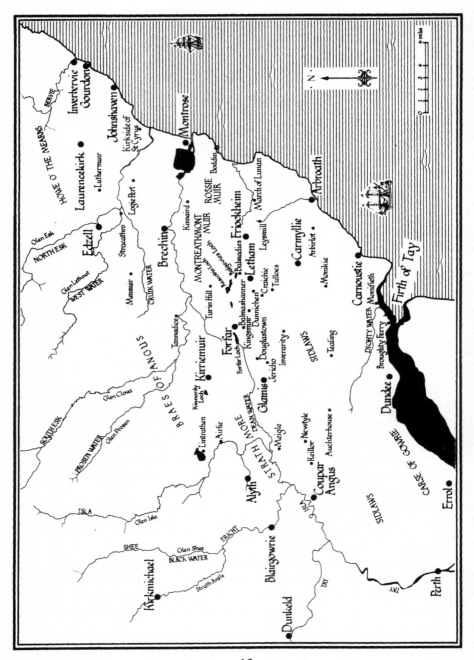

A 1940's contributor "F.W.R." to the local paper suggested that, since "for long it was called Killamoor in local speech, it has to be concluded that the original name in Gaelic was 'Cille Mhuire' - the Church of Mary." Such is certainly the derivation of the name Kilmory, but not everybody agrees it as such for Kirriemur.

Churches dedicated to St. Mary have long been, and still are, in existence in the town, but since they probably belonged to centuries later than the 12th, the balance of opinion chronologically falls on the side of the "Carrou Mor" theory.

Nevertheless, students of history, and place-names in particular, seem to favour, perhaps more by hunch than logic, the "Cille Mhuire" root.

A categorical conclusion is therefore patently impossible!

Why "Thrums"?

To answer the question, "Why did Barrie choose the name 'Thrums' for his supposedly fictional handloom weaving village?" is a little easier!

Variously spelt, thrums threads were used to join old and new webs in the loom, and to repair any broken or imperfect threads.

A Thrums weaver

Being reinforced ("dressed") by starching, they were also used as the loom cords. Bunches of them always hung at each end of the weaver's loom as he worked and a similar bunch still hangs daily beside the giant weaving machines at work in Messrs. J. & D. Wilkie's factory today.

But thrums threads were put to a multitude of uses besides.

The weaver's trousers ("breeks") might well be tied at the knee with them as garters, or his braces ("gallaces"), and even buttons, replaced by them. A watch chain made of plaited thrums was not uncommon, and they were the most popular type of bootlaces.

In his home too they were put to good use, as sponge, mop or duster, and to support his plants in pot or garden. They made good kindling for his fire, and helped mend many a broken tool, barrow or item of furniture. Not only did he tie up his finished web ("wob") with them, but the shopkeeper usually tied up his groceries with them too. Children, always inventive creatures, found no end of uses for them in their play, and altogether they were therefore truly indispensable to the weaving community.

Not much wonder, then, that Barrie chose that name as he, in turn, attempted to weave a tapestry of the rich variety of characters and life-styles which made up such a community.

But although it may be said that Kirriemuir did not make its presence felt in the world until "Thrums" and its author hit the headlines, it had in fact been in existence for some 600 years before then.

It first entered recorded history as long ago as the year 1201, when the Earl Gillechrist bestowed "to the abbey of Aberbrothock (Arbroath) the chapels, lands, tithes, common pasturage and all the pertinents belonging to the Church of Kerimore."

That one of the chapels referred to (dedicated, who knows?, to St. Mary?) seems to have been situated where the present Old Parish Church stands, is supported by the knowledge that a hamlet, known as "the Kirkton of Kirriemuir" grew up around that site.

It is there that our story of the physical and social development of the town begins.

• THE KIRKTON OF KIRRIEMUIR •

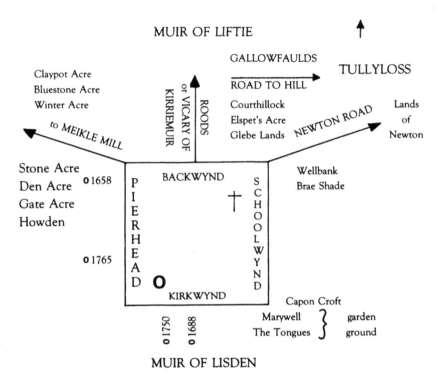

MUIR OF LIFTIE

GALLOWFAULDS

TULLYLOSS

Claypot Acre
Bluestone Acre
Winter Acre

ROAD TO HILL

to MEIKLE MILL

ROODS or VICARY OF KIRRIEMUIR

Courthillock
Elspet's Acre
Glebe Lands

NEWTON ROAD

Lands
of
Newton

Stone Acre
Den Acre
Gate Acre
Howden

o 1658

BACKWYND

PIERHEAD

†

SCHOOLWYND

Wellbank
Brae Shade

o 1765

o

KIRKWYND

o 1750   o 1688

Capon Croft
Marywell
The Tongues

} garden
   ground

MUIR OF LISDEN

† Chapel/Church since 1201
O Tolbooth/Town House since 1604
o Dated Lintels on earliest stone-built properties

The Kirkton was bounded by the present Schoolwynd to the east, Reform Street and St. Malcolm's Wynd (known jointly as the Backwynd at that time) to the north, Seceders' Close and Pierhead to the west, and Kirkwynd to the south.

One of the Celtic cross-slabs found during 1786 excavations in the Parish churchyard, confirming very early habitation of the area.

Immediately beyond these bounds were the Infield acres, with further afield the Outfield acres, or commonties, upon which some of the feuars had the privilege of common pasturage, and others that of "casting fuel, feal, divot and clay." The commonty at the north of the Kirkton was called the Muir of Liftie (now the Northmuir) and that at the south and west the Muir of Lisden (Southmuir, Westmuir and Herdhillmuir). The only relics of these still held in Commonty are the Hill of Kirriemuir (the immediate Superior's rights in which were made over to Kirriemuir Town Council in 1926), and the land between the Gairie Burn and Forfar Road, still known as the Commonty. This was the bleaching green in the days of the weavers, and after that part of it was used as a public drying green.

Where the lock-ups stand in Lindsay Street beyond the top of Sunnyside was once Mortar ground for common use.

The Commonty with 1900's drying green

A 1715 map of this area makes no mention of a Kirkton but only of a "Milltoun" which was situated further up the Gairie towards Kinnordy Loch and centred on the many small mills which used its then more abundant waters. This omission is, to say the least, inexplicable! Little is known about this Milltoun, compared with the volume of documentary evidence concerning Kirriemuir. Apart from church records, title deeds prove conclusively the existence of properties in Kirriemuir prior to 1697. Population figures are available also for the Kirriemuir of 1561 (124 people living in 32 houses) and of 1660 (167 people living in 41 houses).

Houses or Hovels?

These houses were primitive constructions, about which little can be stated categorically, but much surmised. For sure, they would be small, low buildings, probably made of divots or clay with roofs covered in turf or thatch. Doors and windows would be open spaces, unless sacking, hides or planks were put over them. Floors would be the bare earth, with perhaps stone slabs here and there. The fire would burn openly in the middle, with the smoke hovering until it found escape through a small hole in the roof. No home comforts inside either; crude wooden stools, not necessarily a table of any description, the simplest of cooking utensils and pots, and a sackful of straw to sleep on at the end of a hard day!

Bad and bad enough in dry and cold weather, living conditions must have been less than pleasant in any heatwave and diabolical in the wet! With clay turning to mud and thatch rotting, the worn alleys between houses must have been squelchy quagmires, pitted with potholes and puddles. Open drains and sewers complete a picture of altogether foul-smelling and unhealthy living!

While Forfar, Montrose, Arbroath, Brechin and Dundee all date from the early 12th century, not until 1459 was "Kerymure" created, by King James II, a free burgh in barony, "with the power to buy and sell; have bakers, brewers and all necessary providers; a market cross and a weekly market." Only then was the way made open for it to develop into a market town, which it duly did.

Spruce thatched cottages still occupied in Glamis village

Out with clay: in with stone

At much the same time, people began to build with stone, but as late as 1837 "primitive dwellings still thatched with black rotten straw" were said, by a Mr. Robert Millar in his lecture on his early memories of Kirriemuir, to be still standing. But with quarries and forests all around, there was certainly no lack of building materials.

Steam-powered quarrying at Balmashanner, near Forfar

It would appear, however, that scant regard was paid to planning. Rev. James Headrick was moved to comment in 1813 that "the only plan which seemed to have regulated the building of Kirriemuir was a total defiance of all plan."

In 1894, a Dundee gentleman, delivering a lecture to a prominent literary society in London, seemed to agree: "Its houses are all higgledy-piggledy, just as if they had been taken up three or four hundred feet and allowed to be riddled into whatever place they happened to fall."

Clusters of houses around the Parish Kirk

Robert Louis Stevenson's description was later borrowed by Barrie: "irregularly-built little houses squeezed close to the Square like chickens clustering round a hen."

Somewhat haphazardly, then, stone building began.

Early Stone Buildings

As the 17th century dawned, such was general prosperity under James VI that Kirriemuir built its splendid new Tolbooth in 1604. The rounded part at the rear of the Town House in the Square is thought to be the earliest stone building still standing, having survived several riots, and more than one attempt on its life, not least to meet the needs of modern vehicular traffic!

For unquestionable proof of the dates of some of the other stone buildings, we have to look to the five remaining dated lintels dotted around the town. In his "Regality of Kirriemuir" published in 1909, Alan Reid cites several, some of which have disappeared since then.

The Tolbooth of 1604?

Dated Lintels

High up on the gable of the building to the south of the westmost end of Roger's Close off the High Street, is an ornately inscribed oblong stone, with the letters probably T A I P and numbers 16.5.8. If this is in fact the date 1658, then it would suggest that this area of the town belongs to that period. Certainly the narrowness of the lanes and closeness of the buildings is reminiscent of the architecture which did nothing to stop the spread of the Plague, or the Great Fire of London of 1666!

Just to the south and east of the 1604 Town House, in Kirkwynd, is a beautifully recreated stone inscribed "IF 16♡88 BF". These stones are frequently referred to as marriage or nuptial stones, as the initials are thought to be of the couple who got married and had their house built in the specified year. The stones are usually to be found in one of three places: above the doorway; above a fireplace; or above or below a window. Which of these locations applies to the Roger's Close one is not clear! A very small one found in the garden of 92 Glamis Road, inscribed "IBAM 1735" must have been placed above or below one of the very tiny cottage windows.

As regards the initials, it is worth remembering that many Scots women retained their maiden name after marriage, and therefore the same initials. Margaret Ogilvy, Sir J. M. Barrie's mother, was, of course, one such.

To the right of the 1688 Kirkwynd stone, tucked away above the corner shop window is another stone, inscribed (but presently covered over) "J7 IB IR 50", the date being 1750. Thus we can be fairly sure of Kirkwynd's origins.

OLD GAIRIE INN

An 1896 artist's impression of the Old Gairie Inn
(J. Stirton: "Thrums and its Glens")

25

Across the Square, beside the car park and above the side door to the Visocchi's house above the restaurant, is the next stone, inscribed "J7 DW IS 65", carefully restored and replaced during renovation work. To the left of it, the nameplate "Cumberland Close" is attached to the building said to have been the Old Gairie Inn originally. Legend has it that the Duke of Cumberland stayed there overnight on his way back from Culloden (1746). Facts unknown!

Alan Reid records the existence of a dated lintel above the kitchen fireplace, inscribed "JADW 1603". He states that the Inn was in business until 1879, and thatched until about 1895, the favourite venue of mourners after funerals!

As this area of the town, from the White Horse Hotel to Bank Close (formerly Gardener's Close) is to be "rehabilitated" any day now, many of these historical relics may soon be no more.

An unpretentious panel inscribed "Thom and Brand 1764" was, until recently, just barely decipherable on the Barrie's Land side of a house on the corner of the Glengate opposite Gordon Park.

The sixth remaining lintel is in Morrison Street in the Southmuir, about which more presently.

A Town Begins to Grow

With the trend towards stone building therefore well under way by the middle of the 18th century, what brought about the upsurge in the population figures from the 167 people of 1660 to the 670 of 1748 (when some 2634 souls were also said to be resident in the rural areas of the parish, 367 of them in Glenprosen alone!) and the 1584 people of 1792? To find the answer to that, we must turn our attention to the countryside.

The Tannery and Boot factory, Tannage Brae, established around 1750

Stirton's, one of Kirrie's longest-surviving saddleries with the Ogilvy Arms' stabling behind

The Pendicle

Long before anyone coined the phrase "the good life", the people of Scotland lived a very hard life in self-sufficient crofts, called "pendicles" hereabouts. From dawn till dusk they laboured, tilling the soil to grow their basic foodstuffs, grain, mostly oats, potatoes, kail, perhaps turnips and some fruit in their "kailyard". They sometimes were able to keep a cow for milk and meat, and would send the hide after slaughter to the local tannery (in Tannage Brae, in the case of Kirriemuir). Some of the leather could be used to provide their own footwear and working garb, the rest sold for shoe-making in the adjacent boot factory, or to the saddler for transforming into saddle, harness or rein.

Their clothing had to be provided by their own hand. By growing a little flax, enough yarn could be spun, using drop spindles or pirn wheels, to furnish the family with coarse linen clothes, made from material woven by the family themselves, if they had their own loom, or by the local weaver ("wobster"). Many did own their own loom so that, during the winter months, they could eke out their meagre livelihood from the land by selling what they wove.

Angus Folk Museum, Glamis, where time stands still, courtesy of The National Trust for Scotland

Furnishings for the house too were produced in this way - sheeting, towelling, tablecloths and patchwork quilts. The Angus Folk Museum at Glamis recalls these days, and their way of life, admirably, and their book entitled "Angus Country Life" leaves no stone unturned in providing information about every aspect of rural Angus over the centuries.

So it was that weaving had been part of the Scottish scene since the Middle Ages.

As early as the 14th century, the Scottish Parliament had had reason to challenge the "wobsters" for cutting off "ower lang thrumys", "damping" the cloth, and retaining customer's yarn - all of which goes to show that human nature doesn't change very much!

The Wind of Change

But the wind of change began to blow through rural life, in the form of the agricultural revolution of the early 18th century.

Prosperity had allowed many landowners to begin to travel abroad and witness first-hand different methods of farming. For generations, landowners had rented out pendicles on a year-by-year basis, or just strips of land, called runrigs, upon which each tenant farmer could grow what he pleased. Side-by-side, within feet of each other, totally different crops would be grown - corn, potatoes, beetroot, neeps, oats, kail etc. and grown again, year after year. Strips beside a burn, for instance, would be repeatedly flooded; strips exposed to the elements would have the seed blown away or rained away, or the crop uprooted in the wind. Soil became exhausted, "productivity" meagre to say the least.

Enlightened minds saw the advantages of creating "enclosures", fields as we know them, properly drained, irrigated if need be, and protected by dykes, hedges or trees. Soil could be properly ploughed and nourished, and crops planted by rotation and in suitable soil types.

Not only would these methods improve productivity, but also profitability, especially if the landowner were also to be the sole farmer, and pocket the proceeds from his produce himself.

Beechie House, Beechwood, Southmuir, the Almshouse of yesteryear; amid executive housing and "Storyville Residential Home for the Elderly" built in 1989.

Horse and Cart of the 1890's (at Guthrie Castle)

So - out on their ear went many of the tenant farmers and their families, evicted from "their" land and the "tied" cottar's house that went with it!

What were they to do? Here they were - jobless, homeless and penniless, their few possessions heaped on a cart, or strapped to their own backs. Without an income or a roof over their heads, the poorhouse was their fate, unless ....

Rumour had it that there was work to be had "at the weaving", so off they headed for the nearest market town to which materials for weaving with would be delivered. Thus many came to Kirriemuir. Dunfermline and Laurencekirk had similar experiences.

Enter the Loom

And rumour was right, for, following the end of both the devastating rebellions of 1715 and 1745, peace had been restored with France, then a major flax-producing country. Now Scotland could import significantly greater quantities of flax than that which had been home-grown. More work could be had at spinning, weaving, finishing and associated tasks. Boom-time was on its way!

The Saga of the Parish Church

But chronologically speaking, we must pause now to take in an important episode in the town's history, which was excellently detailed in the brochure produced by Kirriemuir Old Parish Church to mark its Bi-centenary in 1988.

Shortly after his induction in 1785, Rev. Thomas Ogilvy, evidently a man of action, was able to convince the heritors of the need to have a new Parish Church built. It was at that time their responsibility, as the major landowners, to build and maintain the Parish Church, and pay its minister's stipend.

The origins of the then existing church building remain veiled in the mists of time. Only Rev. George Ogilvy's short history of the parish in 1748 describes its appearance at all - 100 feet long and 20 feet wide, with two aisles and built, like many pre-Reformation churches, in the shape of a cross.

Nigel Tranter suggests that Kirriemuir's pre-Reformation church may have resembled this one he has sketched at St. Monans, Fife.

The same Rev. George had encountered militant opposition to his Presbyterianism when he had first attempted to take up his charge in 1713. As most of the landowners and their loyal servants were Episcopalians, they had formed a hostile mob to bar his way at Wester Tarbirns. His induction had had to take place at Drumshade, and he could not take up his appointment properly until 1716, after the defeat of the Jacobites. Having got off to such a controversial start, however, his ministry in the end lasted for 55 years!

His successor, Rev. William Eadie, had had his share of troubles too, coming to a sticky end following the weavers' debacle at Cloisterbank in 1783, which will be described shortly.

A new manse had been built in 1774, not terribly well, apparently, as it required extensive repair in 1787! Two hundred years later nevertheless it is still in excellent working order as the Bakery and dwelling house, Manse Close, Reform Street!

By the time Rev. Thomas Ogilvy took the reins, then, a new church was required to meet the needs of the growing town. On September 14th, 1785, the heritors (of whom Mr. Charles Lyell of Kinnordy was the chief) agreed to build one and commissioned the eminent London architect, Mr. James Playfair. The contract signed on October 20th, 1786, stipulated that the new church would seat 1600 and cost £1,249.

Playfair's elegant 1788 Parish Church.

The key was eventually handed over on November 22nd, 1788, public worship having commenced in the new church that September. Even then, faults were found and legal wrangles ensued, before ultimately peace reigned.

The steeple was gifted personally by Charles Lyell (grandfather of the geologist) in 1790, and the bell from the old church, said to have been cast in Rotterdam in 1617, was re-installed. The present bell dates from 1839.

Rev. Ogilvy was to die at the early age of 44 in 1802, but fortunately not before he had contributed the erudite chapter on Kirriemuir to the First Statistical Account of Scotland, which lets us into a few secrets about ...

Kirriemuir - 1792 Style

"Kirrymuir (or Kirriemuir) commonly pronounced Killamuir, is a Gaelic word, and signifies 'Mary Kirk' ". So - categorically - does the forthright Rev. Ogilvy begin!

"No town in the county has a better weekly market. Nine carriages go twice, and often thrice, weekly to Dundee, loaded with the produce and manufactures of the district, and bring from thence flax, sugar, tea, porter (ale), rum, and all kinds of merchant goods ...

"Two annual fairs are held here, in July and October, for sheep, horses and black cattle, and for flax, wool, labouring utensils and household necessities.

"It contains 492 houses, 471 families, 10 brewers who are likewise inn-keepers, 12 retailers of foreign spirits, 3 of wine, about 20 of ale and whisky, 27 merchants, 228 weavers and 1584 souls.

"Two tan-yards have been established here for some time, and a third is erecting. A distillery was begun some months ago" (abolished by 1801) "with a view to establishing a brewery at the same place ... N.B. a brewery here would be of the most essential use to the place and neighbourhood."!

"About 1200 pairs of shoes are made annually for exportation" (in the Tannage Brae Tannery) "and the manufacture of coarse linen is carried on to a very great extent. Osnaburg" (of which more later) "scrim and birdy, to the amount of about £38,000 Sterling were manufactured from September 1791 to September 1792.

36

A journeyman weaver can, with ease, gain 16d a day; a woman 8d at spinning. A mason may earn 1s 8d to 2s, and a joiner 1s 3d to 1s 6d a day. Beef, mutton and lamb cost 3d - 4½d per lb., eggs 3d - 4d a dozen, butter 9d - 11d per 27 ozs., cheese 6s - 8s a stone, and meal 14s per boll." (Modern equivalents are difficult to make, but 12d, i.e. old pennies, made 1s, i.e. shilling, which was equal to 5p when decimal currency came in.)

The minister's stipend was then "112 bolls of victual, two-thirds meal and one-third bear, and £470 Scots - including £50 of communion elements, and £20 for grass money, with a glebe of 4 acres."

The schoolmaster's salary is 200 merks, (a merk was two-thirds of one pound) with a commodious house" (still standing behind "Peggy's Drapery" at the foot of the Roods on the west side). "The number of scholars varies from 60-100. There are two private schools in the town, at one of which the numbers are much the same as at the parochial school. At the other are taught from 20-40 scholars.

The number of poor families which constantly receive alms is at present 19."

Residence of the Parish Schoolmaster until c.1874. The school adjoined the left-hand gable.

In his 1801 amplification of Ogilvy's work, Rev. Alexander Peat comments: "They are obvious truths, that there is no man or woman of decent character, willing to work, who will not find employment; ... men who give indiscriminate charity encourage either idleness or worse. Every parish is bound to provide for its own poor and, besides robbing the poor with whom we stand immediately connected, by our liberality to stranger beggars, we throw away our money, not barely to encourage, but to support the idle, the lazy and the profligate. 'He that will not work should not eat' : Paul." Hmmm.

The Weavers' Society was formed in 1785 to provide support for weavers' families in time of ill-health, and meal at economic prices. Others, such as the Shoemakers' followed, and combined to build the Trades' Hall in Bank Street in 1815 (latterly "Franchi's").

Elsewhere in the town, stone buildings had been appearing in profusion: among them, the Tannery and the Parish School (Roods) around 1750; Seceder Hall (1775); the Auld Licht Manse (c.1781); the Relief Congregation's Chapel (Angus Mill building) in 1792; and the Episcopalian Church of St. Mary in the Roods (Masonic Hall site) provided by Mr. Charles Lyell of Kinnordy in 1795.

By 1801, the employment statistics read:

Clergymen 4; merchants and shopkeepers 30; surgeons 2; schoolmasters 7; farmers 78; innkeepers 10; smiths 12; masons 28; carpenters 50; weavers 515; shoemakers 56; tailors 39; butchers 4; millers 25; bakers 3; gardeners 9; male domestic servants 4; female 96; male farm servants 290; female servants occasionally 251; flax-dressers 18; carriers 14; daylabourers 47; poor from 15-30, and 2 young people at University.

Thus we have a picture of Kirriemuir as a thriving, industrious and developing community at the dawn of the 19th century, attracting to it, among others, swarms of ex-tenant farmers in search of "work at the loom".

All very well - but where were they to live - and work?

A major housing crisis soon developed. All available houses and land in and around the town had soon been taken up - so where to now?

Read on!

CHAPTER TWO

THE WARK O' THE WEAVERS

Mary and Ellenor's Towns

Two significant decisions were made: one, to divide up the Muirs (which in recent years had been causing a lot of trouble, with feuars accused of encroaching beyond the common land on to private land); and two, to make previously privately-owned land available for housing.

Gilbert Meason of Balmuckety was one of those responsible and helpful landowners who offered some of his land for the creation of houses-cum-workshops for weavers.

Since the 1600's, landowners had been giving a Feu to allow a weaver to build his own house, which had to contain his loom and family. The ground was divided into three sections and rotated annually. One section was used to grow flax, one for the family's own use, and one for a bleaching green. Should any of these written conditions be broken, the weaver and his family would almost certainly be evicted. Tough times!

In the early 1820's, therefore, the little communities, or "colonies", of Maryton and Ellenorton appeared, named after the two Meason daughters. Maryton continues to this day, but Ellenorton? Apparently it was re-named, at some imprecisely known date, and for some unknown reason, after the Biblical Padanaram! It certainly had this name by the 1890's, and became associated more with shoe-making than weaving.

Following the division of the Muirs, house-building began on the Northmuir in 1813, the Westmuir in 1815, and the Southmuir in 1826. There is no Eastmuir because the land up the Brechin Road. Newton Parks etc., seems always to have been in private hands.

39

Three Maryton homes here

Hill Road, Northmuir, c.1900

Glamis Road, Southmuir, c.1906

16 Morrison Street, Southmuir, with Masonic connections

At No. 16 Morrison Street, Southmuir, we find the sixth and last of the town's dated lintels. The date here is 1835, sandwiched between the letters D and M. While the significance of the central symbol in the other lintels is not known, although it is understood to indicate something about the occupants of the house, this one is. It is the symbol of the Freemasons, and it has been suggested that this house may have been built by David McHardie who was a draper in the town and a Freemason. It has also been said that the masons actually used the house as their clubrooms at one time. Assuming that only one Lodge is involved, the same group, presumably increasing in membership, may have moved out in to the vacated tannery buildings in Tannage Brae. Eventually they took over the Territorial Force Association Hall in the Roods, built in 1911, now duly inscribed "Masonic Hall."

But let us now venture into one of these weaving colonies for a closer look . . .

Shared gables and chimneys in Henry Street, Southmuir

Buts and Bens

Economy dictated design in these days as in many others. Hence most of the cottages were built in terraces, sharing gables and chimney stacks. Local red sandstone, from the many quarries, such as off the Glengate and up the Brechin Road, was cheap and plentiful, and the woods around supplied the timber, cut to size at the equally plentiful sawmills.

Roofs were on the whole thatched, though some boasted grey stone slates, some of which survive under spreading moss, to this day. Individual feus were surprisingly large, but for a purpose of course. The house would be built to the north of the site, leaving as much ground as possible to be cultivated, kailyard-fashion, under the southern exposure for essential supplies of potatoes and vegetables, plus the compulsory "flax-patch" and bleaching green.

These tiny 18th century South Street windows survived until 1989

Of considerable significance was the size of the windows. As is so often the case, governments have to take the blame! Some enlightened gentlemen saw fit in 1747 to introduce a tax on windows such that, unless you were well-to-do, you could afford only the smallest of panes, and most ordinary weavers were anything but well-to-do. Thus it was that they had to work all the hours God gave of daylight because cruisie lamps, and even the later gas-lamps, gave insufficient light for the intricate work at the loom. When the tax restrictions were lifted in 1798, many of the little windows were blocked up, and larger ones put in. Evidence of blocked-up windows abounds throughout the town. Even 19th century windows were not unduly large because of the cost of glass.

The Newtown Hotel (now "Newton") c.1906

The Rev. Dr. Alexander Whyte, of whom we shall hear more later, was born into one of the Southmuir cottages at 26 South Street in 1836, and once gave a vivid description of their interiors:

"There were rows and rows of weavers' shops in the Newtown (i.e. Southmuir) where I was brought up; generally comprised of a 'but and a ben', the 'but' being the kitchen with maybe a little room as a bedroom or sitting-room. Then at the other end there were four weaving looms. The father would have one and perhaps two

Whyte's birthplace in Fore Row, Southmuir, built also in 1836. As 26 South Street today, much modernised.

daughters would have one each, and the son would have one, or some other person. It has always amazed me how the people managed to live. The father might make twelve or fourteen shillings a week and with a little extra work he would perhaps make sixteen shillings, while the others would have perhaps five, or six or seven shillings. It is amazing to think of the way they turned out and always had a little to give to a good cause, and sometimes - who would believe it? - were able to send their sons to college. But it was done!"

Describing these weavers' houses as they were in the 1860's, a writer to the St. James' Gazette in 1888 described how the floors were not laid, i.e. were only earth, and, where the weaver had only one room, this would contain the loom, two closed-in or 'coffin' beds, a dresser, two tables, one of which could be packed away beneath the other, some chairs and stools. In one corner would stand the wheel at which the housewife or daughter filled the pirns for the loom. "The housewife could not have cleanliness in the house because the threads fastened themselves around everything."

Companionable weaving and pirn-winding

Hanging over the chimney, or beside it, would be the clock known as 'the wag at the wa' because its pendulum was not enclosed in a case. The two windows which faced each other across the room were so small that only a child could have wormed through them with difficulty. They opened with hinges like a door. A hole in the wall of the short passage leading to the dwelling-room would hold a pitcher of water. In the room itself, a similar hole known as the 'bole', the same size as the windows, would hold the family library. The 'saut' bucket stood against the wall.

Where the looms were separate from the living room, they were in a 'shop', i.e. an earthen floored room with only the four looms in it and a long groove hollowed out under each one to accommodate the treadle. Four little windows were arranged along the back wall, with the looms at right angles to them. The windows were low above the ground so that the beams, the long, heavy tubular rolls around which the fabric was woven, could be more easily passed through them directly on to the barrow in the street. The spaces where the looms

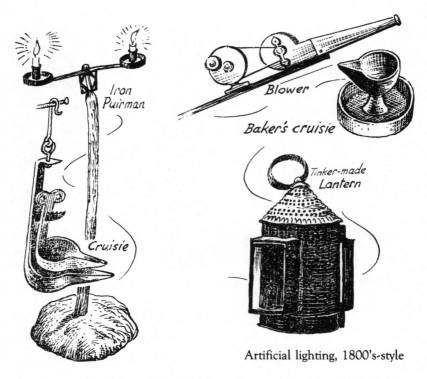

Artificial lighting, 1800's-style

were placed were called 'loom stances' and those could be let to a weaver to build his own loom on, or he could hire the loom which was already there.

Most weavers were 'back-bent' from stooping over the 'wob' from early morning till late at night. Shops were lit only by 'cruizeys' (also spelt 'cruisies'), iron lamps consisting of two spouted ladles which held whale-oil in the uppermost one, allowing the surplus to drip off into the lower one and be re-used. Herd boys sold rushes at ½d a bundle to be used as wicks. The lamp was hung by a hook, or 'cleek', close to the person working.

"Even with three wicks, these gave only a weak light, a 'stime'. At night, the four cruizeys did not give enough light to let you see who was at each loom."

Amazing, indeed! But can you imagine the noise?

They talk about the 'sough of the shuttle' and the 'click and clatter' of the loom, but four of them, all together, all day long in one room about the size of a modern single-car garage, cheek-by-jowl with ordinary family life, through the, albeit 18-inch thick, wall?

Families came economy-size too, each with their part to play in the daily work routine but confined to the living-room by day during the bad weather; sleeping several to a bed of necessity, often squashed into a box bed against the living-room wall. No interior spring mattresses either - chaff or horse-hair for the lucky few.

How did Mum survive? All these mouths to feed and clothes to wash and her only gadgets her hands and simple tools. Water was fortunately freely available - provided you humphed it from the well - but really pure water, from the springs of Culhauk, was not introduced until the 1850's. Wells were everywhere, most folk having one to themselves in their "garden" - but their "garden" also housed the rubbish pit, not to mention the fairy at the bottom thereof, usually known as the dry closet, i.e. a hole in the ground, periodically re-located.

It does not do to dwell too long on the niceties of human survival in these unhygienic - and, of course, illness-plagued - days. The good old days in spirit maybe, but hardly in fact!

Up-The-Stairs

Not all weavers, however, lived in a but 'n' ben.

"Up the town" two-storeyed houses accommodated merchants or weavers and their families, generally thought to have been the better-off ones. Certainly these houses were considered "posher" with their distinctive outside stairs, once so common a feature around the Square, the Glengate and the Roods, but now a rarity.

There seems to have been two ways of utilising these buildings: either the family lived downstairs, with much the same amenities as the cottage dwellers, and the loomshop was upstairs; or vice-versa.

A rare sight today, outside stairs, Barrie's Land, Glengate

Thanks to his writings we know that the house into which J. M. Barrie was born in 1860, was run along the latter lines and built relatively recently. Margaret Ogilvy's kitchen-living room was upstairs, an 'up-the-stair' as she called it, as was the bedroom she shared with her husband and newest babe. Downstairs, one room housed the father's looms and the other was used for spinning, storage of materials etc., and no doubt also contained the box beds in which the rest of the family slept. The loomshop became the family's parlour only once the looms were removed to a separate building in Lilybank. The staircase was always inside this type of house.

Barrie's Birthplace, Brechin Road, today.

West Hillbank's distinctive blocked up windows

An even better example of this type is to be found at Nos. 1 and 3 West Hillbank, the joint back wall of which boasts no less than 8 windows, of which 6 have been carefully blocked up. With a similar number of windows originally also to the front of the property, we have here premises, built by David Orrock, a warper, probably early in the 19th century, in which as many as 16 looms may have been at work simultaneously. The family's residental accommodation was definitely 'up-the-stair'.

Perhaps it is the modern trend towards labour-saving which makes one feel that it must have been much more practical to have the weaver work on street level; after all, looms were heavy things to install, even in parts to be assembled in situ, and beams and reels of yarn, possibly miles of it, no small item to carry. The finished web, all 146 yards of it, can't have been lightweight either!

Kilnbank House and Lane, Glengate

Nevertheless, many workshops are known to have been upstairs, and Kilnbank House was built in 1837 by a "manufacturer", i.e. an employer of weavers, so that he and his family could live downstairs while his weavers worked 'up 'ee garret'. He was magnanimous enough to build a row of cottages in the Lane alongside for his employees to occupy - but there were looms installed there too!

These then were the housing and working conditions "enjoyed" by generations of "Thrums" weavers.

Heichts And Howes

How, then, did the weavers fare as time went on?

Did the boom they enjoyed equal the Klondyke of the gold-diggers, or did they merely make an adequate-to-good living?

As we have seen, their wages were never sensationally high but could, at times apparently, be abyssmally low, for continuing prosperity can never be guaranteed, as, even today, people are learning from bitter experience.

The weaving industry, then, like many others, was subject to "heichts and howes."

Of course, governments are never slow to cash in on a good thing and the Jacobites had been quick to clamp strict regulations on weaving from the outset. They it was who brought in the requirement that every web had to be measured, examined and stamped only if found satisfactory, before being sent to market - after the necessary taxes had been extracted, of course! "Lappers" too were authorised to enter the bleaching yards to satisfy themselves that no forbidden chemicals, or other substances, were being used.

The upper floor of the Town House was a hive of activitiy as the webs were brought there for inspection. Woe betide the weaver whose toil produced inferior quality work! When times were at their hardest, it was not unknown for such webs - anything up to two weeks' work - to be taken out into the Square and, in full view of all, slashed to ribbons, or burned. No wages for that family!

The imposition of these rules was viewed with mixed feelings by the weavers. Where improved quality and, therefore, marketability

The iron yett guards the entrance to the Town House with its basement jail, between 1862 and 1896.

resulted, they had no complaint, but where they were seen as merely pettifogging, they would rebel vociferously against them.

Chance too had its part to play according to the story told about a weaver who, in 1738, somewhat diffidently offered a web which was not the current 'regulation cloth' to a merchant. The latter was amazed to notice its similarity to the popular fabric he had recently seen at Osnabruck in Germany. He urged the weaver to make more, which he did, and "Osnaburgs", so we are told, were thus in production in this area. Since they sold £38,000 worth of them in 1792 alone, that chance was of no small significance. A hard-wearing heavy-duty cotton or linen, it was much used by the militia for horsecloths, canvases, leggings, and the like, and by blacksmiths as aprons.

The poet David Shaw of Forfar was inspired to write these words in "Tammy Treadlefeet":

> "We weaver lads were merry blades
>   When Osnaburgs sell'd weel;
> An' when the price o' ilka piece
>   Did pay a bow o' meal:
> Then fouk got sale for beef and veal,
>   For cash was rife wi' every bodie;
> An' ilka ale-hoose had the smell
>   O' roas'en pies an' reekin' toddie."

Some bonnie sights were to be seen day by day on the Commonty, if Joseph Gordon's "Star of Strathmore" is to be believed:

> "On the bonnie banks of Gairie
>   there is a bleaching green,
> And lovely are the lassies there
>   that bleach their linen clean;
> They kilt their coats, as merrily
>   they tramp the washing skeel,
> And sing like any mavis,
>   nor care nor sorrow feel."

The tree-lined Commonty today, a beauty spot.

David Sands' house in Manse Close, off Reform Street - later a lemonade factory, now demolished. (J. Stirton: "Thrums and its Glens" 1896.)

David Sands

By far the best known Kirrie weaver was one David Sands, a studious and dedicated lad who made his mark on the industry nationwide by inventing a loom in which he made an entire shirt, three of them, in fact. "He not only hemmed and stitched them, without seams, in the loom; he also put on buttons and wrought the button-holes; and, as it was the fashion of the times in which he lived, he put ruffles on the breasts. After exhibiting them among his acquaintances, one of them was sent to the King, another to the Duke of Athole and the third to the Society for Encouraging Arts and Manufactures ... For that, the whole benefit he received was only £5!"

A great achievement in the days of 1772 but at a great price, for the poor fellow died not long after, leaving a grieving widow and a youngest son of only two years of age. His house was said to have been "in the square of houses known as the Corn Yard", which may have been located along the east side of the present Reform Street car park. A building there later utilised as a lemonade factory was claimed to have been his house.

Cloisterbank

Hunger may make good kitchen, but it can distort the truth, and cause people to take up their cudgels on behalf of a cause which may turn out, in the end, not to be a just one. Such was thought to have been the case when, in 1783, following the "Snawy hairst" when the uncut corn, during terrible weather the previous October, had been buried beneath several feet of snow, the weavers decided that the farmers were hoarding the already scarce corn and, in modern parlance, artificially inflating its price to their own advantage. They took it upon themselves therefore to raid the stores of corn, (which they found surprisingly meagre) take their ill-gotten gains into the market-place and there sell it at a fair price, which was then handed over, without deduction, to the owners.

However reasonable this practice might seem to the outsider, it was found more than a little irksome by the farmers, who retaliated by forming themselves into a yeomanry unit of some 100 cavalry and 300 infantry and, armed with pitchforks, scythes and assorted clear-intentioned weapons, prepared to meet their plunderers head on. A daunting conglomeration of Kirriemarians, male and female, faced them at Cloisterbank, just to the east of Westmuir, and in a hail of stones, accompanied with a full orchestral percussion of warlike noises, the yeoman bold took to their heels. Still, justice had to be done and some of the ring-leaders were tried and imprisoned. The Baron Bailie, with power of pit and gallows over his fellow townsfolk, was himself imprisoned for two months for having appeared to give his blessing to the weavers' actions. And, horror of horrors, the parish minister was suspected of bearing false witness and was subsequently found dead, by an unknown hand and in suspicious circumstances, by the side of the road to Forfar!

More peaceful times in rural Westmuir. Cloisterbank is to the right.

1839 Weavers' Riot

As the 19th century dawned, things were looking up in Kirriemuir. Nearly two million yards of brown linen of one description or another were being stamped annually and, since the regulation length of any one web was a mere 146 yards, you begin to get a picture of the extent of the business.

Spinning was keeping the womenfolk in full employment too and the advent of mechanical spinning mills, as near hand as at Douglastown, in 1792 and Glamis in 1806, had greatly speeded up and increased the availability of spun yarn, for finer linens and Holland cloth, suitable for making into sheets and shirts.

But while in 1816 the people of Kirriemuir could boast that more cloth was being stamped here than in any town in Forfarshire except Dundee, by the next year less than five shillings was being paid per web and times were hard. When a glut threatened to aggravate this situation, resourceful entrepreneurs concentrated their efforts on

Selling chickens in Kirrie Square before 1896. To the left, the Sheriff's sanctuary in 1839.

producing products which were thought likely to appeal to the home market, until such time as the foreign market would open up again. A wage drop in 1826 led directly to some people setting themselves up as agents for manufacturers in Dundee and Forfar, a practice which thrived until the end of the century, involving merchants as far afield as London and Manchester.

But when the manufacturers again felt obliged to reduce the price paid per web, the weavers, encouraged by the Chartists, decided to take up their cudgels once more and the notorious Weavers' Riot of 1839 ensued.

Suffice it to say that the weavers took on, first the individual manufacturers, then the Sheriff and 70 constables who had been sent to arrest the ringleaders but found themselves taking refuge in the Town House, then finally, the combined forces of a contingent of soldiers from Dundee and some hefty members of the constabulary. Physical and psychological victory the weavers may have had, but it was short-lived, and some of their leaders were eventually imprisoned. The aforementioned Alexander Whyte's earliest memory was of being awakened in the early hours of the morning by the shouts and jeers which accompanied the sound of marching boots on cobbles as the soldiers led their captives off to prison.

Said to have been a more serious affair than Cloisterbank, it hallmarked the weaving community for all time as one not to be tampered with lightly.

Intelligentsia

It should be remembered, of course, that the weavers were regarded as the intelligentsia of their day - literate, numerate and articulate, and pretty political animals to boot. The Chartist issue was **the** topic of these times and it was not unknown for the weavers to "down tools" and go off to political meetings on the Market Muir to discuss the latest developments.

Likewise, when the weekly periodicals and journals were due to arrive by carter from Dundee, off they would head for town, frequently to the Mills' family home at 17 Bank Street, where, in later years, Barrie was to aver that he had his first introduction to literature.

61

By dint of sheer numbers too, they were a force to be reckoned with. Rev. George Easton's worthy Statistical Account of 1833 states that more than 3,000 people were engaged in the production of linen, with some 1,500 to 1,800 looms at work. He also declares that the influx of people from the land "in search of work at the loom" seemed to be about finished by then.

In 1834, some 845 families were living within the town, that is 3,241 people, and **not** including any of the Muirs!

From hamlet to town indeed!

"Rulers may order and Kings command,
But the power of the people -
who can withstand?"

The Chartists' Banner carried in a march from Dundee to Forfar in the 1830's

CHAPTER THREE

THE WIND OF CHANGE

The March Of Progress

Mr. Robert Millar's lecture had asserted that, "In 1837" (when he was a boy growing up in the town) "the town gave the impression that its inhabitants had not sought to lend Nature any hand by seeking to beautify their little town. Its muddy streets; its crooked wynds; its irregularly-built houses - with their small windows, all of a dull brown colour, and covered with still duller looking grey flags, while a few of the more primitive dwellings were still thatched with black rotten straw."

The South Parish, the steeple-less Kirk of the Southmuir.

In 1860, the new Manse of the Parish Church; in 1989, the Day Care Centre for the elderly.

Nevertheless, by the following year, gas lighting had been introduced to these selfsame streets. Substantial buildings appeared all through the town: Webster's Seminary in 1836; a Quoad Sacra Chapel of Ease (later the South Parish Church), nearby it, off Glamis Road, in the same year; a whole rash of churches following the Disruption of 1843 - the South Free (on the site of the present St. Andrew's till 1903) in 1843; the North Free (present Glengate Hall) in 1846; and the West United Presbyterian Church (Boys' Brigade Hall) in 1853. The new Old Parish Church Manse was built on the Glebe in 1860. A prison for the bad lads of the Southmuir (then still not part of the town) was built in 1853 ("Kirriekut" hairdressers now). The new Cemetery on the Hill was opened for business in 1858, replacing the one in the Parish Kirkyard which was described as having become "obnoxious"!

The Southmuir Prison built in 1853.

Not so obnoxious now, the Old Parish Churchyard.

Kirriemuir Railway Station sketched by David M. Wilson in 1862. (On view in Barrie's Birthplace).

The advent of steam power in the form of the Railway line to Forfar and Dundee in 1854 and the introduction of telegraphic com-
munication began to release this somewhat insular little community
from its relative isolation.

1874 saw Reform Street School built. "The Kirriemuir Free Press"
was established in 1884, and the foundation stone of the Town Hall
was laid in 1885 - sure signs of progressive prosperity.

Wind Of Change: Mark II

The wind of change was making its presence felt again, this time in
the shape of the Industrial Revolution.

For quite some time, it had become obviously wasteful of both
time and energy for so many weavers to be working individually in
their own homes, trundling daily back and forth to the Square to
collect their materials or return their finished work for selling. Webs
were, for years, collected for market in the stone shed which still
stands at the foot of Grant's Pend beside the "Cat's Close". Porters
were employed to do the trundling with their barrows. One such, a
well-remembered worthy, was Chairlie Froster, or Forrest, who served the Southmuir weavers faithfully in this capacity all his life until

Webs were collected in the stone shed beside "The Cat's Close", off Bellies'
Brae, north end. White house occupies site of a former blacksmith's.

67

Window in Thrums, Kirriemuir

Chairlie Froster, astride his famous, and unique, Southmuir barrow.

his death in 1912. So renowned was he that he was featured, sitting on his barrow - the only one in the Southmuir by all accounts! - outside the "Window in Thrums" cottage, on a picture postcard which was familiar to generations of local people. His great-granddaughters, by the maiden name of Herd, still live in the town. He himself lived in Glamis Road opposite the present Co-op grocery.

As well as sharing porters, the weavers decided to share workplaces. Small "manufactories" were set up, where several self-employed weavers worked their own handlooms under one roof. Their requirements were transported by a carter with his horse-drawn cart. Alternatively, "manufacturers" installed the looms and either rented them out to weavers or paid wages to the weavers and pocketed the proceeds from the sale of their webs.

Kirk to Linen Manufactory to Meal Mill: The Angus Mill, Glengate, now closed.

One of these manufactories was set up in the building, built as a Chapel for the Relief Congregation in 1792 but abandoned by them in 1832, better known as the Angus Mill, at the foot of the east side of the Glengate. Mr. George Duke was the employing manufacturer there.

When the Seceders' Church across the road fell vacant following the erection of the West U.P. Church in 1853, the Wilkie brothers put it to use also as a manufactory.

Writing his "Historical Sketches" in 1865, David Allan was able truthfully to record:

"There are from 1,500 to 1,800 weavers in the parish. Of these, the weavers of Ellenortown" - note the name still in use! - "and a few in Marytown, are employed by Forfar manufacturers, and nearly 200 are employed weaving fabrics to supply hawkers. Every description is woven, from a 10-porter scrim or coarse hessian, to the heaviest twilled linen or Dornoch tablecloth. The weavers are in general very expert and a good hand will earn from 9s 6d to 11 shillings a week. There are as yet no power looms in Kirriemuir. Steam has, however, been introduced to turn the machinery of a saw-mill at Southmuir and the corn and flour mills of Meikle Mill."

"Oose" and threads everywhere as the weaver works.

Enter the Giant

No less than three years later, Colonel Kinloch of Logie laid, with Masonic Honours, the foundation stone of the Kirriemuir Linen Works of Messrs. J. & D. Wilkie, where steam power was first utilised. They occupied the prime site, nearest both the water of the Gairie Burn and the railway station.

Hot on their heels followed Messrs. Ogilvy and Stewart with their Gairie Linen Works a little further from the station, on Belly's Brae (contemporary spelling!) "Bellies' Brae" is a corruption of "Bailies' Brae" or "Bailie Street", dating from the 18th century when the Baron Bailies held their Regality Courts in the Town House at its head.

To establish these factories was their solution to the dilemma they found themselves in - between remaining loyal to a well-tried and tested traditional craft, as it dwindled in the face of advancing technology, or remaining competitive by moving with the times. How often has that problem been encountered in the generations since!

Even JMB's father acknowledged the writing on the wall and forsook his loom for a responsible clerical post in one of the new factories, first in Forfar, then, from 1872, in Kirriemuir. As JMB himself later described it in "Margaret Ogilvy", his moving tribute to the woman whose vivid tales of the Kirrie of her youth had so fired his imagination:

"A giant entered my native place in the night and we woke to find him in possession. Where had been formerly but the click of the shuttle was soon the roar of 'power'. Handlooms were pushed into a corner as a room is cleared for a dance; every morning at half past five the town was wakened with a yell, and from a chimney-stack that rose high into our caller air the conqueror waved for evermore his flag of smoke. Another era had dawned".

All those who felt unable to adapt to the faster and more powerful machines were allowed to continue to use their handloom and work their web as before, and, for a while, the best of both worlds was enjoyed. But demand for hand-woven goods gradually diminished

The conqueror waves his flag of smoke over the town and its cemetery until the 1970's.

and the steam-driven looms took over, not least because their products were both good in quality and reasonable in price.

The story of the firm of Charles Hutchison & Sons, as retold in an 1896 booklet produced by the Scottish Home Industries Association (which was formed in 1889 to resuscitate some of the old home industries killed by the introduction of machinery!) says it all:

"From a two-storeyed house in Roods Street which served as dwelling, loom shop and finishing room, Charles Hutchison moved to East Hillbank, where he built himself, in 1834, a larger house and a warping mill of his own. Previously, like many other weavers, he had had his webs warped at ½d each at the common warping mill near his home. At East Hillbank, he added later a small factory or workshop accommodating seven looms. For a time, this was not enough, and webs were again given out to weavers in their own homes, but, by 1896, the factory was once more adequate to meet demand. Mr.

Underfloor drive shafts and overhead pattern-makers: The new era.

Hutchison took his sons into partnership in 1861. They produced first only plain linen but later added twilled linen, diaper towellings and lastly tablecloths which could have a draughtboard pattern, or variations of that -broken dice and guard dice and stripes, plain, broken or guard. Hard-wearing sheeting and, for a time from 1879 on, wincey were produced. Since the introduction of the power loom, it became impossible to find weavers -they were getting old and infirm and were not being replaced. Hours at the factory were shorter and pay better and more dependable. The handloom weaver

Crawford House, a long-time weaving and warping mill.

still had to work from 8 am till 7 pm to earn at best 15 or 16 shillings a week, out of which he had to pay 2 shillings to have his bobbins wound -work formerly done by the wives and children in the days when a woman might rock the cradle while filling her husband's pirns. A baby in these days might have been lulled to sleep by the mother fastening the cradle by a cord to the treadle of her loom."

Charles Hutchison's firm seems to have been one of the last to survive and the imposing Crawford House which still stands on the northern corner of East Hillbank and the Roods, with its distinctive curved glass windows, basement flat and two-storeyed superstructure, with garret, was, almost certainly, his. In the 1980's, hooks remained fixed to both the eastern gable and the top of the garden wall to the south, between which ropes were strung from which the linen was hung to dry after bleaching. It is still said that nothing much will grow in the soil beneath where the lines used to hang.

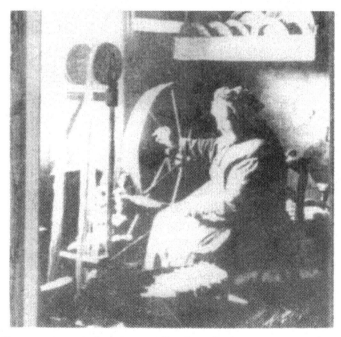

Granny seems to be pirn-winding here by her cottage window.

Alan Reid, author of "The Regality of Kirriemuir" 1909.

Exit Thrums

Alan Reid, in 1909, concluded his chapter in "The Regality of Kirriemuir" on "The Day of the Weavers" thus:

"Here and there, towelling, sheeting and tablecloths may still be seen in the making on the looms so common in other days. But students of Barrie should hasten to make acquaintance with the clumsy wooden machine for they will never rightly or fully understand numerous references made by the novelist till they see it, and its days are numbered."

He was right.

By the onset of the First World War, the handloom was silent and "Thrums" had gone for ever.

Postscript

But what of "the Auld Lichts" who were so predominant in Barrie's writings about "Thrums"? Who were they? What did they believe? How did they come to wield such influence over a community?

Even clerics admit that the history of the church in Scotland is a tangled web of sectarianism, brought about by differences of opinion over Biblical interpretation, rituals of worship, selection of ministers, control of congregations, or relationships between church and state. To some extent, it is a matter of embarrassment, shame even, to the established church that their ancestors allowed such trivialities to divert them from the central issue of the worship of God and emulation of the example of Jesus Christ.

However, it is among such differences of opinion that the Auld Lichts had their origins. The Secession, or Associate, Church was formed, under the influence of brothers of the name of Erskine, as a

The Seceders' first church in Kirriemuir, off the foot of the Glengate, built 1775; later Wilkie's manufactory, the Good Templars' Hall and rehearsal rooms.

The Auld Licht Manse, Brechin Road.

The Auld Licht Kirk in Bank Street from 1807 to 1892.

breakaway group from the Established Church of Scotland, at Gairney Bridge in 1733. Basically they were intent upon preserving the right of church members to choose their own pastors and on resisting all moves towards moderation and innovation, preferring to uphold the principles which had been those of the 17th century Church of Scotland.

After meeting for a while in the barn of Mr. Watson's farm at Shielhill, the Kirriemuir Seceders built their first meeting place in the town, thanks to the generosity of Mr. Arrot, younger, of Dumbarrow, at the lower end of the Glengate, in 1775. Kirriemuir at this time was described as having been "morally bad - almost beyond redemption", but, nevertheless, the first minister of the Seceder Hall charge, Rev. James Aitken, a young man of only twenty when ordained there on 29th December, 1778, soon succeeded in accumulating a membership of 100.

When controversy arose nationally in 1795 over absolute adherence to every word of the Westminster Confession, "no ordinary man", the Rev. Aitken refused point blank to accept the "new light" being cast upon old opinions under the name of the "Voluntary Principles", and clung tenaciously to his "auld licht" ones, the only minister north of the Forth so to do.

His congregation became split on this issue and decided to go their separate ways, the New Lichts retaining Seceder Hall, the Auld Lichts retaining the manse built around 1781, up the Brechin Road, but required to find themselves a new meeting place. Thus they created the new renowned Auld Licht Kirk in Bank Street in 1807. By remaining loyal to original Secession principles, they were within their rights to call that church "The Original Secession Church of Kirriemuir", but, physically speaking, the Original Secession Church in Kirriemuir was the Seceder Hall! Oh, what a tangled web ...

Rev. Aitken served his flock with distinction, preaching three times every Sunday, not one word of his sermons ever being written out beforehand, visiting the homes of his congregation regularly, instructing all age-groups in their faith and helping the poor, sick and out-of-work from his own pocket.

In the year of his death, 1834, another petty controversy was splitting his congregation - namely, whether or not the precentor should continue to read out each line of the psalm before the congregation sang it, a practice necessary in the days of illiteracy but now becoming redundant. Normally totally resistant to innovation, on this one occasion, the Auld Lichts bowed to the march of progress and thus ended the Run-Line Controversy!

In general it appears that the Auld Lichts were a straightlaced lot, rigidly cleaving to uncompromising and Puritanical principles and practices. Tolerance and moderation were unknown concepts to them, sinners being publicly dressed down by the minister and shamed in the face of their fellows. Special sins calling for rebuke included family brawls, wandering the fields on the Sabbath Day, neglect of family worship, frequenting public houses too often without occasion, dancing at 'penny' weddings (where rioting and debauchery lasting a whole week were said to be rife!) and taking the oath of the Masons or any other secret society.

So strictly did they observe the rule that every baby must be baptised on the Sunday following its birth, that it was not unknown for a poor mother to drag herself and her babe to church within hours of their joint discomforts on the childbed, rather than face the ire of the reverend gentleman the next Sunday!

So biased were they against any sect of the church holding beliefs in the slightest detail different from their own, that they would excommunicate any of their own members seen to have associated in any way with one of them. The story is told of a wealthy Glasgow manufacturer who, for having sheltered from the rain in the open doorway of the Tron Kirk throughout its service, was so severely reprimanded by his fellows on the Seceders' Session, that he promptly broke off relations with them and joined with a friend to found a new church of their own!

The security of the Secession Church was threatened somewhat in 1852 by the formation of the Free Church of Scotland, following the disruption within the Church of Scotland in 1843. The new Free Church principles were virtually those of the Seceders rehashed, so much so that the majority of the Seceders' ministers were absorbed by the Free Church.

The new "Auld Licht Kirk"; in Bank Street, built in 1893 on the old site; now the Baptist Church.

Despite the ensuring dearth of true Secession ministers, a succession of them were found to take charge of the Kirrie congregation, none of them, however, able to remain here - for various reasons - more than a few years. The congregation remained steadfast nonetheless and confidently embarked upon the demoliton of the old church and building of a new one. It was the Rev. Professor Aitken of Glasgow, grandson of the original Mr. Aitken - and just as much a stalwart of the Secession movement - who opened the new church on April 5th, 1893.

When Rev. William Cochrane Conn was inducted as its first minister in November, 1897, it was said: "Thus the Auld Licht Kirk of Thrums is in a position to tickle once more the genius of J. M. Barrie." Maybe - but not for long. Mr. Conn was, in time, to transfer his allegiance to the Established Church and Auld Licht principles were themselves to come under pressure as the twentieth century progressed.

Exeunt The Auld Lichts

Rigidity had been both the strength and weakness of the Seceders.

With increased prosperity nationwide, they had attracted more and more of the successful businessman, the self-made man of his day, who could afford to travel any distance to worship in his chosen manner, leaving the poor labourer to walk to the nearest church, usually the Parish.

As these congregations thus became poorer, and less able to meet their customary obligations in education and poor relief, these functions were gradually taken over by the state, and real religious fervour emanated more and more from the Seceders. Using all their available business acumen, they consistently placed their churches on sites with good prospect of capital development and commercial viability, as is clearly seen in their choice of the Bank Street site in Kirriemuir. When the first church on it required to be replaced, shrewd business brains had shops incorporated into the design on street level to help ensure a regular income from rent in particular, to support the congregation. Modern churches could do worse than revive this custom!

Thus a congregation which had risen to an influential, even dominant, position in the community, on the resolute backs of the handloom weavers, began life in its new sanctuary, in 1893, with every confidence that the steam-driven looms in their factories would serve only to consolidate and further their cause. What they failed to bargain for was that the spread of education would so improve literacy as to allow more people to read - and query - the Bible for themselves, and subsequently to call into question, with admirable articulation, their hitherto unchallenged creed and practices.

Bit by bit, petty differences over matters such as rituals of worship, were seen to be just that, and erstwhile hostile denominations agreed to sink their differences and unite. A series of unions followed, into the United Free Church, then the United Presybterian Church and ultimately the Church of Scotland, until, at last, even the Auld Lichts were no more.

FROM HAMLET TO TOWN

LIST OF ILLUSTRATIONS
and their sources

Key to Sources

J.D.A.   Original photography taken by my husband, J. David Affleck

A.D.L.   Old photograph collection of Angus District Libraries and Museums Department.

N.T.S.   Old photographs belonging to the National Trust for Scotland and sketches from some of their publications:

Map - from "Angus Country Life"
Cruisies - from "Angus Folk Museum Guide"

K.O.P.C.   Reproduced from Kirriemuir Old Parish Church's Bi-centenary Brochure

J.S.   Copied from James Stirton's "Thrums and its Glens" 1896

L.G.   From Mr. Lindsay Grewar's personal collection

M.V.   From Mr. Michael Visocchi's personal collection

To all of these, my sincere gratitude.

S.A.

APPENDIX 1

POPULATION FIGURES

Year	Population	Houses	Source
1561	124	32	D.A.
1660	167	41	D.A.
1748	670	187	D.A.
1792	1584	471	U.F.
	(4358 in Parish)		
1801	421		M.G.
1824	3363		D.A.
1825	5056		D.F.
1834	3241		3rd S.A.
1836	4000		D.A.
1911	3776		K.F.P.
1911	3829		3rd S.A.
1921	3408		K.F.P.
1921	3498		3rd S.A.
1951	3570		3rd S.A.
1961	3485		3rd S.A.
1968	4000+		3rd S.A.
1981	5000+		Census

NOTE ABOUT POPULATION FIGURES

The accuracy of these population figures is difficult to assess, as they come from a variety of sources. Obviously, physical areas included in headcount and other criteria varied considerably. I quote them for interest only.

The sources from which they come are coded thus:

D.A.: David Allan's "Historical Sketches" 1865
U.F.: First U.F. Church 150th Anniversary Book
M.G.: Modern Gazeteer 1808
D.F.: Pigot's "Directory of Forfarshire"
3rd S.A.: Third Statistical Account of Scotland pub. 1977
K.F.P.: Kirriemuir Free Press 16 Sep. 1971

APPENDIX II

CHRONOLOGY OF KIRRIEMUIR BUILDINGS

1604	Tolbooth
1658	Roger's Close - lintel
1688	Kirkwynd - lintel
1697	(Early building on site of Franchi's)
1700 app.	School in Schoolwynd - ruinous by 1784
1700 app.	School Bellie's Brae - sold 1797
1735	Cottages at Muirhead of Logie before Beechwood - lintel
1750 app.	(Tannery) - Mitchell's
1750 app.	(School and) School Master's House, St. Malcolm's Wynd/Roods - sold 1875
1750	Kirkwynd - lintel
1764	Glengate Houses - Thom and Brand plaque
1765	Pierhead/Crofthead - Visocchi's lintel
1774	Old Parish Manse, Reform St. (till 1860) - now Dewar Rhind's
1775	Seceder Hall
1781 app.	Auld Licht Manse
1786	Old Parish Church
1792	Relief Chapel - now Angus Mill
1795	(St. Mary's Episc. Church, Roods till 1902) - site Masonic Hall - also Lyell Burial Ground
1807	(Auld Licht Kirk, Bank St. till 1893) - site F.E. Baptist Church
1816	Trades Hall - 1832 conversion into church - U.P. Church - ex. Franchi's
1813	Northmuir weavers' colony
1815	Westmuir weavers' colony
1820	Southmuir weavers' colony
1828	Tallest Tenement - longtime Commercial Hotel - now Co-Op., High Street
1833	Star Rock, Roods
1835	Commonty acquired - bleaching green
1836	Webster's Seminary
1836	Chapel of Ease - South Parish - Chapel of Rest, Lawson's - Urray Kitchens

89

1836	Alexander Whyte's Birthplace, 26 South Street
1837	Kilnbank House and Lane
1838	Town lit by gas - gasworks previously built ?
1843	(South Free Church till 1903) - site St. Andrew's Church
1846	North Free Church - now Glengate Church/Hall
1853	Southmuir Prison - now hairdresser's, Glamis Road
1853	West U.P. Church - now B.B. Hall, Glengate
1854	Railway opened.
1854	Pure water supply from Culhawk introduced
1854	(St. Mary's Episcopal Church School, Roods - closed 1927 - demolished 1986 - now St. Anthony's Church)
1858	Hill Cemetery opened
1860	Old Parish Church Manse, Glebe
1863	Almshouse established - Beechie House, Southmuir
1867	Leslie, Tailors, established - now Mearns
1869	"Kirriemuir Observer" founded
1869	Wilkie's Factory opened
1872	Ogilvy and Stewart's Factory opened
1874	Reform Street School - closed 1977 - site Lyell Court
1884	Birse & Robb ironmongers established - now hairdressers, St. Malcolm's Wynd
1884	"Kirriemuir Free Press" established
1885	Foundation Stone of Town Hall laid
1887	Tennis Club established
1890	King Edward Place built
1893	Free Evangelical Church (site Auld Licht Kirk) - Bank Street
1895	Police Buildings, Reform Street
1896	South Free Church Manse (St. Andrew's)
1896	Town House became Post Office and Chemists
1897	Parish Council Chambers
1903	South Free Church - now St. Andrew's Church
1905	St. Mary's Episcopal Church, Whiteside
1906	Bowling Green, Brechin Road
1910	Webster's Seminary enlarged
1911	Territorial Force Assoc. Hall - now Masonic (site first St. Mary's Church)

CHRONOLOGY OF BUILDINGS (contd...)

1913	Library and Courthouse added to Town Hall
1926	Hill acquired
1928	Wilkie Shelter erected on Hill
1930	Cricket Pavilion and Camera Obscura, Hill
1930	Vert Maclean Cottage, Glebe Road
1931	First Electric Street Lighting
1952	Fire Station, Glengate
1954	New Webster's Seminary - later High School
1963	Barrie's Birthplace and Museum opened
1972	Peter Pan Statuette erected, Glengate - restored 1983
1977	Health Centre, Tannage Brae
1977	Northmuir Primary School and Hillrise
1986	Library extension and modernisation
1987	Strathearn's new Funeral Parlour, Roods
1987	Lyell Court Sheltered Housing Complex, Reform Street (school site)
1987	St. Anthony's Catholic Chapel, St. Mary's Close (site St. Mary's School)
1990	Sports complex, swimming pool and extension to Webster's High School

The Little Red Town
and JMB

Part Two

The J. M. B. Connection

CHAPTER FOUR
JAMIE

"In Memoriam JMB"

On Thursday, 24th June, 1937, pressmen from all over the world, and people from all walks of life, streamed through the streets of Kirriemuir.

Like some sombre river they followed in the wake of the hearse which bore to his last resting place James Matthew Barrie.

Born 77 years previously in the relative obscurity of the Brechin Road tenements, he had died, whether he willed it so or not, world-renowned as an author and playwright. Such was his fame that, some time prior to his death, he had been offered a burial place in the Poets' Corner of Westminster Abbey. This he had gratefully acknowledged but graciously declined, stating clearly his desire to be buried where his heart lay, beside his family on the Hill of Kirriemuir.

Thus it was that London had to come to Kirriemuir.

"London" took the form of Barrie's long-time friend, now ex-Prime Minister, Ramsay MacDonald; his personal secretary and confidante Lady Cynthia Asquith and her husband, the Hon. Herbert; General Bernard Freyburg VC, much-wounded and exceptionally

The Press have, as always, the best vantage point as Barrie's funeral procession travels from St. Mary's Church down the Glengate and along Bank Street, past the Mills' bookshop.

Ex-Prime Minister Ramsay MacDonald among the mourners.

brave First World War hero, much admired by Barrie; his solicitor and adviser Sir Reginald Poole; and, of course, many, many leading names from the world of the theatre of the day, among them one of Barrie's favourite leading ladies, Elisabeth Bergner and her actor/director husband, Dr. Paul Czinner.

From a' the airts of town and country too they came: the one and only Sir Harry Lauder, Scottish entertainer extraordinaire; Sir David Percival Wilkie, fellow Kirriemarian, by then eminent Professor of Surgery at Edinburgh University, and Lady Wilkie; several representatives of Scotland's Universities, many of which had bestowed honours upon Barrie - Sir Thomas Holland (Principal and Vice-Chancellor, Edinburgh), Mr. Neil McLean KC (General Council, St. Andrews), Very Rev. Dr. Harry Miller (St. Mary's College, St. Andrews) and Dr. Calder (Glasgow): and friends of past and present or their representatives, such as local GP Dr. Robb, son of his late boyhood friend Jamie, ironmonger.

Barrie's extended family too were well represented: his four nieces, the Misses Lilian and Mollie Barrie, Mrs. Smart and Mrs. Philip; his cousins, Mrs. Singer and Mrs. Henderson; and his three surviving adopted sons, Peter, Nicholas and Jack Davies.

Wreaths came from famous and unknown alike: Gladys Cooper, Elisabeth Bergner, Nova Pilbeam and Hilda Trevelyan, leading actresses all; Lady Tree, whose husband had had Her Majesty's Theatre in London built; Irene Vanbrugh and Mr. and Mrs. C. B. Cochran (the impresario); Lord Lyell of Kinnordy and his mother; Lady Langman, Balintore; Kirriemuir Town Council; Kirriemuir schoolchildren; Mrs. Thomson, occupier of Barrie's birthplace; and former schoolfriends.

The simple service in St. Mary's Church was conducted by the current Rector, Rev. H. G. Rorison, and the former Rector, Rev. Canon Philip, whose wife Ethel was one of Barrie's nieces.

The praise consisted of three ageless favourites of the Scottish church: "O God of Bethel", "The Lord's My Shepherd" and "I to the Hills will lift mine eyes".

Crowds of onlookers, many arriving in the town that day by train, bus and motor car, filled the streets. Schoolchildren from Kirriemuir and Forfar lined the driveway up to the Cemetery from the Brechin

One last journey past his Brechin Road roots.

Road, where the cortege had appropriately passed by Barrie's birthplace, then still tenanted by Mrs. Thomson, and anything but spruce in its outward appearance.

Eight men, some more distinguished than others, as reflected the varied aspects of Barrie's life, were the pall-bearers who laid him to rest beside his parents, his brother David, his sister Jane Ann, and the two sisters who had died as infants: Messrs. Alexander O. Barrie and Barrie Smart, his great-nephews; Hon. Bruce Ogilvy, representing Lord Airlie whose family had been friends and admirers of Barrie for decades; Provost J. H. Joiner of Kirriemuir, a friend as well as official of the town, who, along with his wife, had earlier entertained Ramsay MacDonald to lunch in their house which was then called "Marguerita Villa", now "Rosegart", in Victoria Street, Southmuir; Mr. John F. Mills, proprietor of the "Kirriemuir Observer", father of today's local reporter, W. B. Mills, who retains with pride his father's cord card; Dr. A. K. Mill, long-serving GP in Kirrie; Sir James Irvine, Principal of St. Andrews University and friend since Barrie's election as Rector thereof; and the surgeon Sir David Percival Wilkie who had been a frequent London visitor in recent years.

As the "Kirriemuir Free Press" of July 1st, 1937, commented: "Sir James loved simple things. His funeral, removed from garish pomp and pageantry, was marked by its simplicity. This would have pleased him, had he been there to see it. Thrums gave him the homecoming he would have wished -sober, decent, God-fearing, and not overdone."

True indeed, but neither would Barrie's wry sense of humour have failed to contrast such attention being paid to his final departure from Mother Earth with the total lack of attention paid, except by his fretting mother, to his earlier, bold departure from Kirriemuir in 1885!

Crossroads

That had been a crossroads in his life when, spurred on by his success with some of his early pieces about the Auld Lichts, he had packed his bags at Strath View, put his money (all £12 of it!) and his determination in his pocket, and set off, a little man with, at 24 years of age, high hopes of hitting the big time in London.

That decision was to prove worthwhile, for within three years he would have the art of writing where he wanted it - at his fingertips - and his "Auld Licht Idylls" would be selling like hot cakes in book form, soon to be followed by their sequel, "A Window in Thrums".

Thus he was to put Kirriemuir once and for all, as many have said, on the map of the world.

But stop! We are going too fast!

If we are going in this little volume to try to show clearly and in detail just how close and lifelong were his ties with his hometown, then we must first turn back the pages of his life's diary to the very beginning.

Flashback to Jamie

Six of the eight children she had already borne were still alive when Margaret Ogilvy, with the help of a midwife whose surname was Matthew, gave birth to James Matthew Barrie on May 9th, 1860.

That same day, we are told, she took delivery of six hair-bottomed chairs, intended to have pride of place in the parlour she was soon to have - for the first time in her life - once her handloom weaver husband, David Barrie, moved his loom out of the downstairs room into adjacent sheds in Lilybank.

Although large, they were a close-knit family with a mother who, despite a full and busy life, took time with her children, telling them endless stories such as children the world over love to hear, of the days when she was a girl. She cared for them all tirelessly, taking great pride in her ability to 're-cycle' their clothes, by making them down and re-modelling them as often as necessary.

The tragic death of their brother, David, on the eve of his 14th birthday, affected the whole family deeply and permanently, none more so than their mother, whose devastation was to remain with Jamie all his life like a sore which would not heal. To her, David was the boy who never grew up - an image of no mean significance in Jamie's literary mind, which had begun to develop long before he was twelve.

Barrie's Birthplace as it was in 1895 - its drabness relieved somewhat by flower-boxes

Margaret Ogilvy, a bonnie woman in 1867.

Of his own admission, attempting to recall the details of his first six years, up till the death of David, was all "guess-work". Since he spent his holidays from school in Kirriemuir over a good number of years, many of the activities and escapades attributed to the "boyhood in Kirriemuir" period did not necessarily take place during that early spell of continuous residence in the Brechin Road, which, after all, ended when he was just eight.

Putting on plays in the wash-house with his friend Jamie Robb, and charging their chums the famous "preens, bools or a peerie" (pins, marbles or a top) for admission, must have taken place before he was ten, because his parents moved to Forfar in 1870. Little could they then have guessed of how that wash-house would, in later years, be on the receiving end of a status and significance somewhat disproportionate to its original basic function!

Regular attendance at the South Free Church (where St. Andrew's Church now stands) was an integral part of Jamie's upbringing, as it had been of his father's. On her marriage, Margaret Ogilvy had transferred her allegiance there from the Auld Licht Kirk. The dis-

That famous first theatre, with the Lilybank Mill behind.

covery of the beauty of his hometown and its environs was a continual process, with the Den and Caddam (otherwise Caldhame) Wood favourite haunts for family walks or boys' "adventures". His love of the Hill, its views, and the cricket played on it, grew with him as did his pleasure in the art of fishing in the rivers and lochs of the glens.

His education was entrusted, once he was six, to the Misses Adam, who had what was called a "hanky" school at 24 Bank Street. This nickname derived from the fact that pupils were required to bring a handkerchief upon which they would have to kneel when prayers were being said. Later he went to the school attached to the South Free Church. When big brother Alexander was settled as Classics Master at Glasgow Academy, he offered to supervise his younger brother's further education, and give him a term-time home with himself and their sister, Mary. The thought of going to live in the rapidly expanding and industrialised city must have been a little awe-inspiring for an eight-year-old country lad. But, though he might

The South Free Church and school (1843-1903) where St. Andrew's Church now stands in Glamis Road.

never have admitted it, escaping from the oppressive atmosphere of his home since David's death, must have been much healthier for him. His own account, in "Margaret Ogilvy", of his childish attempts to console his inconsolable mother is full of pathos. He seems to have emerged from this with a feeling of obligation at all times to make up for her loss and expiate his own guilt at having survived. Wise minds have suggested that this experience at the age of six, deprived him of the rest of his childhood. In contrast to David, he had to grow up too soon. It seems almost miraculous that he also emerged with a lively sense of fun.

J. M. BARRIE IN HIS EIGHTH YEAR
Photographed at Glasgow.

Off to Forfar

So, in August 1868, he left Kirrie for the first, but no means last, time. He would be home perhaps for the week off at Christmas and certainly during the six-week summer break - no Easter holidays in these days! But home became Forfar in May of 1870.

Having watched Wilkie's power-loom factory rise brick by brick, David Barrie had come to realise that that way lay the future and took the chance, at the ripe old age of 56, to start work in the office of Laird's Linen Works in Forfar. Since 'commuting' five miles each way daily was unheard of in these days, the family moved to a house in Forfar, in a lane called Limepots, now Canmore Street.

There they remained for two years, until Mr. Barrie was offered the post of Clerk in charge of the Yarn and Manufacturing Department of Ogilvy's factory on Bellies' Brae. David Ogilvy, Margaret's minister brother, had bought "Strath View" for his own future retirement and first of all let the top floor of it to the Barries. Later they occupied the whole house. Alexander Barrie also eventually spent his retirement there.

He had a considerable influence on Jamie's future in many ways, not least by his own character, example, tuition, advice and financial support, but also by the changes he made in his own career.

After the Education Act became law in Scotland in 1873, Alex. was designated a suitable candidate for this new educational species, to be called "Her Majesty's Inspectors of Schools". He therefore left Glasgow Academy to undergo further training for these new tasks, and Jamie was able to join the family in Forfar and attend its Academy for a while. When they returned to Kirrie, he went back to the South Free Church School just along the road.

JMB, aged 11, at Forfar Academy, seated first on left - 1871.

The Happiest Days Of His Life

By now, Jamie was fascinated by comics, "Penny Dreadfuls", writing his own episodes of the serials on occasions when his copy was late arriving. His pleasure in being back on his native heath was great, but short-lived, as, with Alexander soon established as H.M.I. of Dumfries district, he was before long despatched there to resume his education at Dumfries Academy.

Older now than when he first set off for Glasgow, this prospect seemed to him more like one of the adventure stories from his comics come to life, and he left Kirrie, again, in the autumn of 1873, in a mood of confident expectation.

Fortunately, this mood turned out to be justified. All students of Barrie agree that these next five years were "his happiest". There was hard work, and plenty of it, but also lots of cricket, football, fun, fishing and writing -and a growing interest in all aspects of the theatre.

First on left in back row this time, at Dumfries Academy, 1874.

105

JMB in his favourite fishing hat "captured" in 1912.

Fishing and walking seem to have been his main preoccupations back in Kirrie for the holidays, catches and distances being logged in his diaries. In 1876, he reckoned he had walked 245 miles in all - in six weeks.

During his last two years at Dumfries, which town also later honoured him with its Freedom, he penned his first articles, immature and inexperienced, of course, a novel and a play, copies of which were to be shown back to him, to his chagrin, in later life!

University now seemed the next path chosen by Alexander (now married) and his parents for Jamie to follow. The choice fell upon Edinburgh, where by now Alexander Whyte from the Southmuir, lifelong friend and fellow-student of big brother Alex, was preaching at Free St. George's, and might deputise as "guardian". He had been in Glasgow at the same time as Alexander and Jamie and the trio had enjoyed many a long and pleasant walk together.

His last summer at home was one of mixed emotions: sadness that his "childhood", especially the one he had lived through his imagination and games, was finally over; pleasure from the familiar faces and places, fishing, walking, writing, reading. Above all, the desire not to let his mother down impelled him to go forward, and off he went, "up" to Edinburgh in 1878.

Grind

His much-quoted diaries sum up the next four years as "grind, grind, grind", but his persistence, and Alexander's generosity in paying his fees, was rewarded, and he graduated with an M.A. in English Literature.

He was, by then, convinced that literature was his game, but writing it, not reading. In this, he had to disappoint his mother who still hankered to have a son in the ministry, but this only intensified his determination to succeed in **his** chosen career. In her latter years, his mother was to read all he wrote with interest and with pride - a slight contrast from the early days when she hid his anonymous Auld Licht pieces in case anybody would realise who had written them!

Not long after he came back to Strath View (he always wrote it so), Jane Ann, the sister who was to be her mother's lifelong nurse/companion, at no small cost to herself, noticed an advert in "The Scotsman" for a leader-writer on "The Nottingham Journal". His application, backed by effusive references from Alexander Whyte among others, was successful, and once more he left Kirriemuir behind.

The only trouble was, he maintained, that he hadn't a clue what a 'leader' was like, never mind how to write one! Most amusing is his description in "Margaret Ogilvy" of his mother and Jane Ann unearthing old copies of newspapers from drawers and under carpets so that he could devour their leaders. Perhaps it is not surprising, however, that, in a commercial re-appraisal of "The Journal", it was decided to dispense with his services! So he returned to Strath View in October, 1884, jobless. What did mother say about that, one wonders?

The Scotch Things

Undaunted, and indeed doubly motivated, he began sending to a variety of publications, a variety of articles, generally unsigned. A few years later, Dr. W. Robertson Nicoll, founder and editor of "The British Weekly" and a major influence on his future career, was to suggest he use a pen-name, and so "Gavin Ogilvy" appeared, author of, among others, "An Edinburgh Eleven".

Sabbath observance among the Auld Licht community at "T'nowhead".

Following the advice still given to aspiring authors, viz. to learn the art of stringing words and sentences together by first writing about familiar subjects, he optimistically submitted, still anonymously, to the "St. James Gazette" an article entitled "An Auld Licht Community". They published it in November, 1884! Its editor, Frederick Greenwood, another subsequently influential figure, soon requested "more like that Scotch thing". As 1885 dawned, "An Auld Licht Funeral", "Courtship", "Scandal" and "Wedding" followed one another like the feet of a centipede scurrying to London - and Barrie decided he should follow suit.

His mother was appalled at the whole idea, visualizing him lying languishing in some gaunt garret or, worse still, on the dreaded benches of London's notorious parks. But, for once, unaffected by her concern, he packed his bags - as already described - and took the overnight train to London, the prototype, in his own words, of "The Scotsman on the make". The date was March 28th, 1885.

We need not go into a blow-by-blow account of his first three years in the big city. Suffice it to say that, by dint of much "grind" of the kind he relished, and a "certain grimness about not being beaten", he had well and truly cut his writer's teeth by the end of them. He had made tentative steps into the world of the novel, never really to be his forte, but most of all, he had persuaded Hodder and Stoughton to publish his "Auld Licht" articles in book form.

He spent the Christmas period closeted in "his little room to the left of the porch in Strath View" polishing up, "Auld Licht Idylls". It arrived on the bookstalls in April, 1888, and Kirriemuir was on the way to worldwide recognition as "Thrums".

On the left, Strath View. Across Glamis Road, the South Parish Church and to its right, "The House on the Brae".

CHAPTER FIVE

ON THE UP AND UP

East, West, Hame's Best

One gets the impression that many people believe that, from the moment Barrie became successful, he turned his back on Kirriemuir and its people, as if, in some way, he had taken all he wanted from them and was now moving on to bigger and better things.

In fact, over a number of years he chose to come back for spells of varying lengths, both to keep a weather eye on his mother's health and to have peace and inspiration to write. Scotland, and Angus in particular, would always be a place where he could "recharge his batteries" and whenever his family needed him, he would be there. As we shall see, while his body might have travelled the world over in its lifetime, his heart forever remained bound up in the land of his birth.

A Window In Thrums

He spent six months at Strath View from the autumn of 1889 until February of 1890, and that year both holidayed in Glen Clova and worked at home on "The Little Minister". It was during that spell that Jane Ann and he are said to have begun to persuade people that "the house on the brae" containing **the** window in Thrums was the cottage across the road, thus diverting attention away from Strath View itself. Much has since been made of that particular piece of fiction! The actual window through which "Jess looked at the world as through a telescope" was in the gable end of the tenement next door to Barrie's birthplace, where lived Mrs. Addison, 'Bell Lunan' to her friends, of whom Margaret Ogilvy was a lifelong one.

111

"The House on the Brae": today "A Window in Thrums".

During a brief summer visit in 1891, he learned with delight of the engagement of his only younger sister, Maggie, to Rev. James Winter.

Sadly, when again at Strath View in May the next year, he was to learn of Winter's death through being thrown from the very horse which Barrie had previously given him to help him get around his scattered parish. Here again guilt feelings led him to cosset Maggie to the point of over-protection. He continued to keep a watchful eye on her during her forty-two year - and happy! - marriage to her late fiancé's brother, the kindly William Winter.

Dunn's shoe shop was demolished c.1910. The Jamieson family (iron-mongers at the High Street end of Jamieson's Close) lived in the upper flat.

In April of that year, 1892, Arthur Conan Doyle and Barrie took a stroll around the roup of the contents of the Auld Licht Kirk in Bank Street about which he had written so much. Since the pulpit, precentor's desk and pews were laid out in lots along Bank Street, behind and in front of the shoe shop building which then occupied its junction with the High Street, this was indeed a curious occasion. Small wonder Conan Doyle was seen taking photographs!

By the 1930's, Bank Street contained (L to R) The New Auld Licht Kirk, Franchi's and the Albion Stores, all but taking over W. B. Mills' bookshop.

According to the local paper of the day, Barrie bought the precentor's desk and some pillars and pews. In the Birthplace today there is on display the paper knife he is said to have made from some of that wood.

Barrie was back again in 1893, both in the spring - to write - and in September to make his first public appearance in his hometown since becoming famous.

The occasion was the Bazaar being held to raise funds for the replacement Auld Licht Kirk. His speech to declare it open in the Town Hall, while lengthy, was not particularly memorable, apart from his expressed concern as to "what Gavin Dishart might have to say about there being a bazaar to do with his church".

He had to come back again in December because his mother was very ill and did not leave till he was satisfied that she was well on the way to recovery.

Mary Ansell and JMB in 1892.

Marriage

When Barrie returned to Strath View the next spring, he caught a chill which soon developed, in his always vulnerable chest, into pleurisy and pneumonia. Without modern antibiotics, these were death-inviting diseases. Hardly surprising, therefore, that Miss Mary Ansell, the delectable actress to whom he had been secretly engaged (pending mother's approval?) came hot-foot to his bedside to nurse him.

Apparently the worst illness he was ever to suffer till his last - and he did not enjoy the best of health - he made a slow but thorough recovery and was well enough in mind and body to be married to Mary by his uncle, Rev. David Ogilvy, in the drawing room at Strath View on July 9th, 1894. For the good of his health, the venue chosen for their honeymoon was Switzerland.

After some days at Strath View the following March, and another ten in August because his mother was once more ill, the next visit to Kirrie was by far the saddest of the many sad ones to come.

In contemplative mood in 1895 - before his mother's death.

Double Blow

A telegram reached Barrie and his wife, on holiday for the second time in Switzerland, informing them of the sudden and totally unexpected death of Jane Ann. One of her regular letters had arrived not long before the telegram and given no hint that she was unwell. Perhaps she had become so accustomed to being worn out that she did not notice any deterioration, such as the presence of malignant disease should have caused.

Realising how this news would devastate his mother, the Barries left immediately for home, a journey of three days' duration. By the time they arrived, his mother too had been dead for some twelve hours. She had not appeared to comprehend when Alex. and his sisters had attempted to tell her what had happened. She had simply wandered through the house, finally asking for the robe (also now on display in the Birthplace) in which David had been christened, a frequent comforter to her in times of depression. Then, turning her face to the wall, she too had passed away.

Side by side they were buried, on Friday, September 6th, 1895 - which would have been her 76th birthday - in Kirriemuir's hillside cemetery. Barrie had a new headstone made so that her name should be above those of his infant sisters and David.

J. B. Greenwood of Manchester was inspired to write the following tribute to them both, but especially the devoted Jane Ann:

The inseparable Jane Ann Barrie and Margaret Ogilvy.

117

"Jess and Leeby"

O Ruth-like constancy, all praise above!
O ceaseless ministry of watchful care!
That gave its all, of precious things and rare,
And even life itself laid down for love.
Herself death-stricken, she kept death at bay;
Safe-guarding, with her own, that honoured life
Which nurtured hers: then, worsted in the strife.
Went, as her herald, up the heavenly way.
The unconscious mother knew not **here** the price
Of that love-tending, in its martyr strength,
Knew not the inverted order, the changed tryst,
Nor that her "Leeby", lone in Paradise,
Watched, listening, for her coming: till at length
Hand knit with hand, they knelt before the Christ."

A dreadful blow, this, and one which was to stop Barrie from wanting to come anywhere near Kirriemuir for many a long day.

Strath View was shut up altogether, his father going to live with his only remaining unmarried daughter Sara, and his late wife's brother, Rev. Dr. David Ogilvy, to whom Sara was both adopted daughter and housekeeper. The trio stayed first in Motherwell, then in Edinburgh.

"Margaret Ogilvy" appeared on the streets in 1896 to a mixed reception -variously branded "exploitation" and "sentimentality". Those who had known her personally kept their own counsel. As for Barrie, it seemed to be something he just had to do.

Spreading Fame

During these latter years of the century, Barrie's fame was spreading far and wide. His journalistic novels were selling well - "The Little Minister" alone sold 24,000 copies in 14 months.

Agents here and in the USA were realising his potential. His introduction to the renowned impresario Charles Frohman in 1896 was of monumental significance, as he staged all Barrie's major theatrical successes on both sides of the Atlantic for the next twenty years. It was he who transformed "Peter Pan" into a magical, theatrical extravaganza.

It was also Frohman who launched the play of "The Little Minister" in New York in 1897, where it received over 300 performances. Later it was made into a film, starring Katharine Hepburn as Babbie.

Mind you, when in 1898 it was given its first performance in Kirriemuir, albeit with a different cast from the New York production, it was not exactly hailed as a howling success! Perhaps the New Yorkers were less bothered by the phoney Scots accents of the all-English cast! Barrie himself later spoke of it disparagingly as a play. Nevertheless it earned him a cool £80,000 in its first ten years!

Kirrie Again

By 1898, Barrie felt able to return to Kirrie, having cycled over from his holiday house at Grandtully on the Tay. He stayed overnight with the Lyells at Kinnordy. In September 1899 he returned with his wife and several relations when Strath View was again temporarily open.

Perhaps, while sauntering around the Kirrie shops during that visit, he noticed David Young's High Street shop selling "Thrums Rock", Duncan's grocery selling "Thrums Whisky", A.P. Mill in the Roods selling both "Thrums" and "Little Minister" cigarettes, and Burnett's selling their "Thrums Make" of boots? He couldn't have failed to see J. Dow & Sons' "Thrums Grocery Store", and may even have bought a copy of James Stirton's book, "Thrums and Its Glens".

Recognition at last!

Sadly, it was bereavement which brought him back again in 1902 when his father, 87 years old, was knocked down by a horse and cart in the High Street, and died on June 26th. It had been planned that he, Sara and Dr. Ogilvy would now move into Strath View for their remaining retirement and he had come on ahead. The Barries attended the funeral but JMB's grief seems to have been much less than for his mother. His father was nonetheless proud of his achievements, as a letter preserved in the Birthplace confirms.

David Barrie, proud father.

Sara and Dr. Ogilvy did move in, but not for long, as Sara died in November 1903 and Dr. Ogilvy in 1904. More funerals; more links with the past severed. Barrie was not to be back in Strath View until after Alexander, who inherited it, moved in for his retirement with his family in 1907.

That visit in March was very brief, as his close friend Arthur Llewellyn Davies was by then seriously ill and Barrie's historic commitment to "stand by his wife and children forever" had already been made. When Mrs. Sylvia Llewellyn Davies also died, aged 43, three years later, Barrie adopted their five sons - George, Jack, Peter, Michael and Nicholas. They were his "lost boys" and the inspiration for his magnum opus, "Peter Pan".

He saw Alex. again for a few days at Strath View in September, 1908, on his way back from a fishing and walking holiday at Callander.

Arthur Llewellyn Davies and his five sons in 1905. (The Lost Boys: Andrew Birkin)

The Kirriemuir Herald of January 28th, 1965, reproduced this picture of the Winston Churchills on honeymoon at Airlie Castle.

"What Every Woman Knows"

That same month, far away in London, a little history with a Kirrie connection was made.

On September 3rd, one Winston Spencer Churchill, recently elected M.P. for Dundee, took his fiancée, Clementine Hozier, to the London première, at the Duke of York's Theatre, of "What Every Woman Knows".

Nine days later, at their wedding, in the Church of St. Mary's, Westminster, Bishop Welldon said:

"....There must be in the statesman's life many times when he depends upon the love, the insight, the penetrating sympathy and devotion of his wife. The influence which the wives of our statesmen have exercised for good upon their husbands' lives is an unwritten chapter of English history, too sacred to be written in full.... May your lives prove a blessing each to the other and both to the world."

It must have seemed as if Barrie's play had been written with them in mind.

By October 9th, Mr. and Mrs. Churchill were honeymooning at Airlie Castle because, of course, Clementine's mother was a daughter of the 10th Earl of Airlie and her grandmother, the then Dowager Countess, was, at that time, châtelaine of Airlie Castle.

Clementine had in fact been confirmed in the Episcopal Church of St. Mary, then situated where the Masonic Hall in the Roods, Kirriemuir, is now, on November 6th, 1898.

By the time Bishop Welldon's prophetic words were being quoted again at Clementine Spencer-Churchill's funeral in Westminster Abbey, on 24th January, 1978, the world knew without a doubt just how true they had been.

This memorial fountain to Captain Scott and Dr. Wilson was erected in Glen Prosen, where they planned much of their ill-fated expedition. A cairn has since replaced the fountain, which was demolished in a motor accident.

Success and Sadness

Never far away, trauma was soon back at Barrie's door.

His wife confessed her love for Gilbert Cannan, a man 20 years her junior and on October 13th, 1909, a decree nisi was granted. The drawing room at Strath View would now join the bedrooms in holding bitter-sweet memories for him.

Ironically, on the very day of the divorce, the infant Peter Scott was being baptised, in the understandable absence of his Barrie godfather. For this, Barrie would again compensate, perhaps even over-compensate, in later life. Peter's famous explorer father, Captain Scott, would ask him only a few years' later, in the poignant letter found with his body in 1913 in the frozen wastes of the Antarctic to "be good to my wife and child. Give the boy a chance in life . . . . He ought to have good stuff in him." As a naturalist and artist, Sir Peter Scott certainly lived up to expectation. He remained a staunch and active champion of all things "green" right until his death in 1989.

Barrie's involvement with the Davies' boys, combined with a considerable workload arising from having several works in preparation and production simultaneously, kept him fully occupied until the 1914 war. It is worth remembering that "Peter Pan" had alone grossed half a million pounds by 1906! Many much-needed Scottish holidays were enjoyed, but none in Angus.

The death of big brother Alex., to whom he owed so much, brought Barrie back to Kirrie in July of 1914, for another slow journey past the Brechin Road Tenements to the Cemetery. Now he would see to it that Alex's widow and children could remain secure in their home.

Tragically, both their sons were killed in action in 1916, leaving their four sisters surviving. They at least outlived their uncle and were able to be present at **his** funeral.

The Big Time

The war years brought many more sadnesses to Barrie as to the rest of the nation. In particular, he grieved over the deaths of young George Davies in action and of Charles Frohman when the Lusitania was torpedoed, both in 1915.

But they were followed by a full decade of "the big time" as Barrie could never have envisaged it. As other biographies fully detail these years, it is necessary only to select a few highlights to give the flavour of the period.

Sir JMB on his election as Rector of St. Andrew's Univesity, with Earl Haig, 1922.

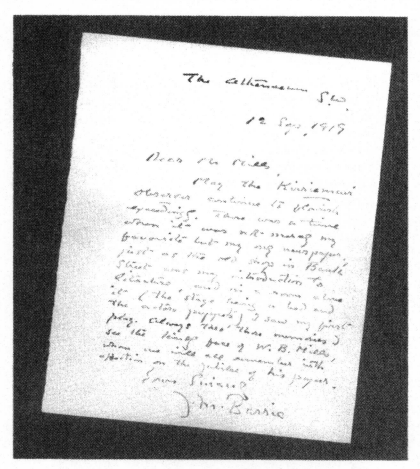

Honours were heaped upon him, academic and civic: an Honorary LLD from St. Andrews' University in 1898, followed by another one from Edinburgh in 1909; a Baronetcy in 1913 - enter Sir James Barrie, Bart.; the Order of Merit and the Freedom of St. Andrews in 1922; the Freedom of Dumfries in 1924, of Jedburgh in 1928 and of Edinburgh in 1929.

Memorable speeches marked these occasions, not least his Rectorial address on "Courage" at St. Andrews in 1922. Perhaps it received such acclaim because it was agonised over for days - his secretary, Cynthia Asquith, records that it took her until 4 am on the morning of its delivery to hand-write the 8000 words he finally decided upon!

It was not unknown during these years for several of his plays to be packing in huge audiences at various London and American theatres simultaneously. "Quality Street", "The Admirable Crichton", "Dear Brutus", and "Peter Pan" were revived year after year, long before the royalties from the latter were made over to Great Ormond Street in March, 1929.

Imagine the status such an author would enjoy today!

And yet the Kirriemarians of the day were, for a long time, reluctant to acknowledge JMB as their own!

Such was the hurly-burly of his life, then, that visits to Kirriemuir became few and far between for a while.

But that it was not altogether out of his thoughts is borne out by the fact that, in September 1919, he took time to write to his old friend, John F. Mills, to congratulate him on the Jubilee of "The Kirriemuir Observer". It was in that letter that Barrie acknowledged having been introduced to both books and the theatre in the Mills' home at 17 Bank Street.

Time to put that Mills family in their place in both Kirrie's and Barrie's stories.

The Mills Connection

James

Born sometime around the dawn of the 19th century, James Mills was a plasterer to trade and an avid reader and collector of books. In the days before public libraries, he took pleasure in sharing his books with all who showed interest in them, and lent, and gave away, lots to many different people, not least among them the boys Alexander Whyte and James Barrie.

In later life, Alexander Whyte would recall "sitting in old James Mills' kitchen among the Chartist weavers who were awaiting the arrival of the Dundee carrier who brought them their weekly parcel of Radical papers . . . I can never forget my indebtedness to him, who provided me with so much good literature, when books were rare and dear".

17 Bank Street, the Mills' family home; later the Doctor's home and surgery; now the Book and Coffee shop of the Baptist Church.

James Mills was also the Kirriemuir correspondent for the "Dundee Courier".

William Black

James' son, the "kindly-faced" William Black Mills was born in 1836 (the same year as Alex. Whyte) and took his father's love of books a little further. He established a "Book, Stationery and Printing" business at 17 Bank Street. There he sold books and a few other things besides - wallpapers, fishing tackle, concertinas, accordions, microscopes and board games - and operated "at moderate charges a circulating library of 500 books".

In 1869, he founded Kirriemuir's first ever newspaper, "The Kirriemuir Observer and Braes of Angus Reporter", printed and published originally on the first Friday of every month at Bank Street. The first issue was gratis, paid for by advertisements from local businesses - one of the main reasons for setting it up in the first place. Later it appeared weekly at the cost of ½d.

Mr John F Mills bids Sir Harry farewell.

The kindly-faced W. B. Mills

Mills' bookshop before 1896 when the Town House outside stairs (and urinal!) were removed.

In that first issue of October 1st, 1869, he announced that he was shortly to open "that shop at top of High Street lately occupied by Mr. William Christison" as a "Fancy Goods Emporium". It would sell tobaccos, pipes, cigars, work boxes, writing desks, toy books, Bibles, school materials, fancy goods and stationery. Since by the 1880's, 17 Bank Street was being lived in by the local doctor Dewar, all business must have been transferred to the Square sometime in the interval. That shop became renowned as a bookshop and stationers only. Home for W. B. Mills and his family had become 4 Anderson Terrace by 1892, probably earlier, simultaneously with the sale of Bank Street.

John Ferguson

W. B. Mills died in 1904, by which time his youngest son, John Ferguson Mills, born in 1874, was well rooted in the business. Following from his boyhood habit of frequenting the Mills home in Bank Street, JMB proceeded to visit the new shop and its new proprietor who, although 14 years his junior, grew to be greatly liked and respected by Barrie over the years. He never failed to call in at the shop whenever he was in town and a meaningful friendship and regular correspondence developed between them. John F. took on the role of Kirrie correspondent to Barrie (as well as to the "Courier"!) and kept him in touch with local happenings. He would send him the paper and any new publications he felt would be of interest to the exile.

Over the years, John F. was to count Scott Skinner and Harry Lauder among his friends and regular correspondents too, and to earn a considerable reputation as an expert on Burns.

To the written history of Kirriemuir he made particularly significant and invaluable contributions. He produced the first Guide Book to Kirrie, entitled "Through Thrums", since by its publication date of 1896, the town had become known as such. It was packed full of history, as were his many contributions to Alan Reid's "Regality of Kirriemuir" of 1909. Once "Barrie-mania" set in around the world (though not necessarily in his hometown!), John F. was consulted by just about every researcher and aspiring author on the subjects of Barrie and Kirriemuir.

Changes all around the bookshop between 1896 and 1910 when the shop at mouth of Bank Street was demolished.

Sir Harry Lauder in Kirrie Square in the 1930's.

A dedicated and meticulous professional journalist, John F. had a keen eye for history in the making, and spared no detail in his articles, all of which continue to be a mine of vital information to the present-day researcher.

Married in 1916 to Margaret Campbell, a cousin of Archibald Campbell, at one time proprietor of both the Airlie and Ogilvy Arms Hotels, John F. had only one child, a son, born on 13th October, 1917, and named after his own father, William Black Mills.

W. B.

By 1932, formal education was over for this young W.B. and he was in full apprenticeship as a journalist to his father. Together they kept the "Observer's" flag flying, though now from the westmost end of the ground floor of the Town House, since Albion Stores had bought over their High Street shop (which is now the ironmonger's). Their printing presses had long been in Roger's Close, at the Crofthead end, behind those of James Norrie, Ltd. They continued to sell books and papers from the Town House and Barrie's last few calls were paid there.

More and more, young W.B. took the reins, and the bulk of the journalistic work was his. During the Second War, his regular features of news from home and abroad, and interviews with young Kirrie lads home on leave, were very important to all Kirrie readers with folks away abroad.

In 1949, partly because of the scarcity of newsprint, James Norrie amalgamated the two papers, the "Observer" and the "Free Press", which had dated from 1884. "The Kirriemuir Free Press and Advertiser" became the sole newspaper, and W. B. continued faithfully to report for it. He also wrote much of the text of the series of Guide books to Kirrie produced by Norrie's until the late 1960's.

Since that "Free Press" "died" in 1974 (twenty years after his father's death), W.B. has reported for every Kirrie paper that has existed under any title, nowadays the "Kirriemuir Herald" (whose predecessor had co-existed for some time alongside the "Free Press"), sister paper of the "Forfar Dispatch".

Now the fourth and last generation of Mills to be the Courier cor-

Home of "The Kirriemuir Free Press" 1884-1974.

respondent, W.B. has acquired in 57 years of detailed, accurate and sensitive journalism, an encyclopaedic knowledge, particularly of Kirriemuir people, which will never be equalled. His admiration for the more illustrious of them remains undiminished and Barrie could ask for no more passionate an advocate than him. He cherishes two dreams -one, to see Barrie more recognised and commemorated, perhaps through school prizes, in his hometown and, two, to see one of his grandchildren, by his three children, follow in his journalistic footsteps.

This year of 1989 has seen the first dream realised, with W. B. personally handing over the W. B. Mills J. M. Barrie Shield to its first winner at Northmuir Primary School, in June. Just a few days earlier, he received word that he had been awarded the M.B.E. for his services to journalism. That this honour was richly deserved has been proved by the hundred of messages of congratulation which have flooded into his home.

W. B. Mills, Esq., M.B.E., "Mr. Kirriemuir", still going strong in 1989.

Last of a line he may be, but one thing's for sure - no four men ever made greater contributions to the recorded history of their home-town than did these Mills, over more than 150 years.

Author's Footnote:

Sadly, this year of 1989 also saw the death of W. B. on 11th December. As Rev. John Stevenson said at the packed memorial service in the Old Parish Church on 16th, "Already the streets of Kirriemuir seem emptier without him."

As previously mentioned, W.B. retained with pride his late father's pall-bearer's card from Barrie's funeral, which event, along with the other great Barrie events of the 30's, he recalled in detail. It is to these that we shall now turn our attention, as we enter the last phase of Barrie's life.

CHAPTER SIX

THE ULTIMATE ACCOLADE

Nostalgia

Barrie's thoughts were again turned to Kirrie when he heard in January 1921 of the death in Hampstead of that other book-loving friend, Alexander Whyte.

Alexander Whyte, Moderator of the Free Church of Scotland 1898.

Suffice it in this book to say that, but for Barrie's meteoric rise to fame, that Alexander might well have been recognised as Kirrie's most illustrious son. For, from the humblest of origins in his birthplace at 26 South Street, he had risen through the ranks of the ministry of the Free Church of Scotland to become its Moderator in 1898, and subsequently Principal of New College.

Be that as it may, they too had kept in touch and Barrie had in fact been sole guest at what turned out to be Alexander's last birthday dinner, just a few months before his death. No doubt some of their conversation on that occasion had been nostalgic for their joint youth in Kirrie. Certainly Alexander's death set Barrie's heart a little further on the road back there and he resolved to return as soon as possible.

But life - and death - again got in the way.

May of 1921 saw the tragic drowning at Oxford of Michael, his favourite Davies protegé, a devastating blow from which Barrie never really fully recovered.

Relentlessly his professional life continued, so that it was not until February of 1928 that he eventually made it back to Kirrie.

It was the death of his brother Alexander's widow which summoned him then but he took the opportunity to renew acquaintance with some of the companions of his early years, among them James

Birse and Robb's shop in St. Malcolm's Wynd, sometime after 1885.

138

Sir J. M. Barrie coming up Bellies' Brae with Miss Jean Bruce, February 1928.

Robb, by now a successful ironmonger in the town. His firm, Birse and Robb, was established in 1884 and situated in St. Malcolm's Wynd opposite the Airlie Arms, where the Hairdresser's is nowadays.

He took time to thank the Bruce sisters for all the care and compassion they had lavished on his late sister-in-law, their neighbour, and to visit J. F. Mills' shop for a chat.

Out walking with "Robb" in Caddam Wood, they recalled the secret whistle they had used in their adventuring days and somehow Barrie's nostalgia for his roots emerged with a vengeance from its hiding-place.

139

In June of that same year, Robb visited him in London, bringing with him the gift of a Kirriemuir canary, then also called Robb. He returned with a letter to the Town Council offering them the gift of a cricket pavilion for the Hill, venue of the many cricket matches Barrie had so enjoyed as a boy.

In response to that offer - and not the other way round, as many people seem to think - said Town Council in turn offered him the Freedom of Kirriemuir. The fifth such honour bestowed on him, this one meant most.

Arrangements were eventually completed and he travelled north, without, for once, a heavy heart.

Sir James and Mr. Robb at Kirriemuir Station, June 1930.

Freedom At Last

On his arrival at Kirriemuir Station (long since submerged under Marywell Gardens), Sir James Barrie, Bart. - somehow the only appropriate nomenclature on this occasion - was greeted by a large crowd of well-wishers, headed by James Robb, in whose home, "Eastfield" in the Brechin Road, he was to stay during his three-day visit.

In the course of the Friday, they went out for a motor-run round some of their old fishing haunts. At Memus, they called in on the schoolmaster, Mr. David Volume whose father had given Sir James his first lessons in fishing, then returned to Kirrie via the Braes of Kinwhirrie and Lintrathen.

Saturday, June 7th, dawned bright and sunny and blossomed fittingly into a glorious summer's day.

Lunch

The first of the day's events was a private luncheon in the Town Hall at which Sir James was the guest of the Town Council.

The company included Provost Peacock, the Earl of Airlie, Mr. David Smith (at 30 years of age, already the Town Clerk and proven to be efficient, which was as well, as he had to make most of the arrangements for the day!), Bailies Doig and Moncur, Councillors Dunn, Barrie, Paterson, Inglis, Irvine and Barry; Mr. Wilfrid Smart (nephew), Mr. Barrie Smart and Mr. Alexander Barrie (grand-nephews); Mr. James Robb, ex-Provosts Wilkie, McNicoll and Moir; Drs. A. K. Mill and Sillars; Messrs. J. A. Carnegie, Wm. Doig, Geo. Webster, Charles Melvin VC, F. Thomson, J. S. Bruce, C. C. Proctor, Charles Macartney and Arthur Mailey (the Australian cricketers), A. Lowson, P. Lindsay and John F. Mills.

Mr. David Smith, Mr. James Robb, Sir James Barrie and Provost H. E. Peacock outside "Eastfield", Brechin Road, June 1930.

142

Sir James Barrie accepts freedom from Provost Peacock, June 7th, 1930.

The Burgess Ticket

For the subsequent Freedom ceremony, the Town Hall, and its platform, were crowded. More VIP's: The Earl and Countess of Airlie, Sir Torquil Munro and Lady Munro of Lindertis, Colonel Stuart Fotheringham of Fotheringham, Sir Harry Hope of Kinnettles, M.P. and Lady Hope, Sir John and Lady Ogilvy Wedderburn, Mr. and Mrs. J. D. B. Ogilvy of Inshewan, General Sinclair Maclagan of Glen-queich, Mr. and Mrs. G. M. Wedderburn of Pearsie, Mr. William Carnegie of Glasgow, Mr. James McLaren, London, Dr. Percy Wilkie, Edinburgh, Mr. and Mrs. George Dundas, Mr. and Mrs. Alex Smart, Mr. and Mrs. D. Forman ... etc. etc.

Provost Henry E. Peacock, recently retired dominie of St. Mary's School off the Roods (where he had been since 1884!) and an articulate and cultured man of letters, no mean patron of the arts locally - presided.

143

The presentation silver casket, showing the town's motto, Strathview (on left), the Town House and Peter Pan.

He paid tribute to Sir James' writing skills - imagination, expression, characterisation - his philanthropy and sympathy towards the needy in society, and his abiding love for the land of his birth.

Then the Town Clerk read aloud the Burgess Ticket after which Sir James took the oath and signed the "Lockit Buik". In presenting the ornate silver casket, the Provost assured Sir James that it contained, not only the Burgess Ticket, but also the heart of Kirriemuir.

Cheering greeted this remark and continued when Sir James rose.

"My Provost, my Lord, my Magistrates, my Town Council, my ladies and gentlemen - for you are mine as no other gathering can be and I am yours as I can never be to any other gathering - you have done me so much honour, my heart is full today.

It is very little I have done but even though it had been much, I would have thought it of no avail, if, when I came back home, I felt that my people did not like me. You make me very proud and very happy ...."

After referring to his Kirriemuir canary back home in London, who would want to know all about the day's happenings, he paid tribute to the two men "who were the biggest influential force in Kirriemuir in my boyhood - James Donald and David White, the first two literary men I ever knew."

In concluding, he thanked "My Provost and Kirriemuir from my heart for the great honour you have done me." Following the toast of "The New Burgess", the audience stood to sing a rousing "For he's a jolly good fellow" before partaking of a Cake and Wine Banquet. Thereafter, all moved off in procession to the Hill.

Charles Melvin 1914-18 War V.C. is second in line during fencing-off work on the Hill, June 1930.

A Hill of Memories

Thousands - yes, thousands - of people were milling around on Kirrie Hill as Sir James arrived to the strains of "See, the conquering hero comes", played by the Town Instrumental Band.

Accompanied among others by the Provost, Town Clerk and James Robb, he stood on the Pavilion verandah before microphones which would record his every word for all the world to hear and, in front of cameras which filmed his every gesture for "Movietone News". Actually, as was his way, he delivered every word with his hands firmly anchored in his pockets!

"It is easy to make a speech anywhere else, but here, on this Hill of memories, to people who are more like me inside than any other people are - I tell you, I would rather go in to bat over there against the West of Scotland's bowling."

But make one he did, recounting some of his boyish exploits, and telling of the letter he had received from Robert Louis Stevenson in Samoa, describing how RLS had, at about 18 years of age, gone on a fishing expedition on the Noran, and had stayed at the Airlie Arms.

Messrs. Smith and Peacock accompany Sir James to the Pavilion.

Then, as is so well known, he told of the secret whistle Robb and he used to use to reassure each other that they had got safely home from their nocturnal adventures and of how they had both rather sheepishly recalled it during Barrie's 1928 visit. "I think that is largely how it comes about that I offer you this pavilion."

Mr. Frank Thomson, architect of the Pavilion, then presented the key to Sir James, who opened the door amid loud cheers.

There then followed the famed cricket match between the West of Scotland and the Allahakbarries, who included the Australian Test cricketers, Macartney and Mailey, and Barrie himself as 12th man: non-playing. The Allahakbarries won by 6 wickets and 38 runs.

Messrs. J. F. and W. B. Mills were not the only ones to notice that, later on in the afternoon, while the game was still in play, Sir James and Robb slipped quietly away into the Cemetery to pay their respects at a certain graveside.

Hands in pockets, Sir James amuses his audience of V.I.P.'s outside the Pavilion.

Lord and Lady Airlie and family listen intently to Barrie's speech on the Hill. The curly-haired young man in the light coat is the Hon. Angus Ogilvy, godson of Sir James - some years before his marriage to Princess Alexandra!

Old Friends

On the Sunday, Sir James visited Strath View where several of his relatives were staying with his niece, Miss M. O. Barrie, for the weekend. He called in also to see Miss Margaret Addison, his oldest friend in Kirriemuir, and Mr. and Mrs. David Thomson, the then occupants of his birthplace. Photographers recorded each one of these otherwise private calls!

In the afternoon, he took his leave, motoring to Downiepark as the guest of the Earl of Airlie, who came in to Kirrie with Macartney and Mailey to collect him.

He finally left from Forfar Station on the 9.15 p.m. train to London on the Monday - tired, but happy, as they say.

Sir James visits the tenants of his birthplace, Mr. and Mrs. Thomson.

On the Hill of Kirriemuir

Cricket was a popular spectator sport on the Hill. Picture may have been taken at the Allahakbarries v West of Scotland match on June 7th, 1930.

Lawn Tennis, Edwardian-style, at Balnaboth House.

One Last Visit

Three years later, he was persuaded back to Kirrie for what turned out to be one last visit. The occasion this time the Town Band Bazaar.

A lot happened, that visit, most of it so well-known as not to require lengthy repetition here.

Yes, this was the time when he had rented Balnaboth in Glen Prosen for the month of August; when he had a constant stream of house-guests, including Ramsay MacDonald, still Prime Minister, with whom - another insomniac - he talked well into the "wee sma' hoors"; when he visited the Airlies more than once, when he entertained the then Duke and Duchess of York and their two Princess daughters to tea; when they invited him back to Glamis Castle for Princess Margaret's third birthday party the next day; when she uttered the never to be forgotten line concerning a small gift with

Sir James proudly displays his newly-acquired clarinet. Lady Cynthia Asquith, his secretary, is on the extreme right. Town Band Bazaar August 26th, 1933.

Sir James Barrie savouring Glen Prosen 1933.

which she was particularly thrilled, and which he enthusiastically admired, "it is yours **and** mine"; which led to his using the line in "The Boy David" and drawing up a contract to pay the Princess one penny royalty each time the line was performed - a duty which was fulfilled sadly by Cynthia Asquith when Barrie was dying.

Pressmen, photographers and admirers from far and wide dogged his every footstep that visit - at last the prophet had become recognised in his own country. A mixed blessing though, for one whose health was not all it might be and was more in need of a rest.

Still, as promised, he turned up to open the Bazaar on August 26th, in aid of the Town Band. Again the Town Hall was packed. Provost Peacock's welcome was warm and sincere, recalling his last visit, the audience's response enthusiastic.

With his slow, sardonic and deliberate delivery, hands once more in pockets, Sir James launched into an enthralling speech which must have lasted well over half an hour. (It certainly did when it was brilliantly re-enacted by Mr. Christopher Hartley of the National Trust for Scotland as part of the concert to mark the Centenary of Kirriemuir Town Hall, on Wednesday, 18th September, 1985.)

He recounted his enchanting encounter with Princess Margaret.

He regaled them with anecdotes about his Kirriemuir Kanary, both with a K, apparently the bane of his life, whom he had hopefully left behind in London.

Then said Kanary seemed to appear up in the rafters of the Hall and start to put up bids on behalf of some of the dignitaries present for the clarinet, which had been sent to Sir James by Miss Georgina Deuchar, whose father had played it at the inauguration of the Town Band in 1861.

Much hilarity was enjoyed by all, until finally the clarinet was knocked down by Barrie to himself for £50. Forthwith he presented it to Provost Peacock on behalf of the town. It remains to this day a treasured exhibit in the Birthplace.

A memorable occasion indeed, and a fitting high note on which to take leave.

155

The crowded scene in Kirriemuir's Hill Cemetery, June 24th, 1937. Simultaneously 600 people were attending an open-air memorial service in the Quadrangle of Edinburgh University. On Wednesday, June 30th, the Archbishop of Canterbury gave the address at another packed memorial service in St. Paul's Cathedral.

Sir James himself later wrote of how much he had enjoyed this August visit, how much good it had done him, and how "sweir" (loath) he was, for once, to return to London which had, for so long, thrilled and satisfied him.

Perhaps he left, feeling that, at last, he had been forgiven for his earlier satirical pieces about his hometown and its people, and that he had finally been acknowledged by his "ain folk".

They indeed turned out in style to honour him four years later.

Which is where we came in.

"If I also live to a time when age must dim my mind, and the past comes sweeping back like the shades of night over the bare road of the present, it will not, I believe, be my youth I shall see, but hers ...." ("Margaret Ogilvy")

Perhaps the popular and prolific local poet of the day, Norval Scrymgeour, spoke for all Kirriemuir when he wrote "Hame's Best".

"Hame's Best"

It's weel oor lad comes hame to rest
In the quiet place he lo'ed the best,
Awa' fra Lunnon's glare an' din,
An' amang his couthie kith and kin.
Fond e'en wi' warm tears will fill,
When he's at hame upon the Hill.
At the wee window on the Brae
He'll ken the faces worn an' wae -
Faces that smiled on him lang syne
When a' o' life for him was fine -
When, rinnin' hameward frae the Den,
He saw the clock on stroke o' ten.

Bring back oor lad frae Lunnon toon,
For he's oor ain, oor clever loon.
Bring him whaur Caddam Woods are near,
An' his chum's whistle he may hear;
Let him lie quiet upon the Hill,
An' let him be oor laddie still.

Aye, bring him back, for he is oors,
An' mak his bed 'mang Kirrie flo'ers.
He's Margaret's loon, an' he maun be
Wi' his ain fouk for company.
Where Jess an' Babbie, an' the lave
Will aye be near his bonnie grave.

For lang the warld kept him awa',
It made oor laddie rich an' braw.
But it was Kirrie that he lo'ed.
An' o' its lad was Kirrie prood.
Weel did we ken he'd come again
To see the Brae, the Hill, the Den.

An' noo he comes to gang nae mair,
An' Kirrie's heart is fond an' sair:
Aye, fond an' sair, but happier still
To hae him back on Kirrie Hill.
Nae title, fortune, fame whate'er
Could please oor lad like Kirrie air.

*****

TAILPIECE

Gone, But Not Forgotten

In 1960, the Centenary of Barrie's birth was recognised in Kirriemuir with a Festival of events from May to September.

Highlights included a production of "Dear Brutus" by the local amateur Dramatic Club, with the professional actors Barry Sinclair and Sarah Churchill starring as Mr. and Mrs. Dearth, in May and Kirriemuir Amateur Operatic Society's presentation - with spectacular scenery - of "Wild Grows the Heather", the musical version of "The Little Minister", in September.

Similarly, in 1985, "Anniversary Celebrations Eighty-five" ("ACE" for short) celebrated both the Centenary of Kirriemuir Town Hall and the 125th Anniversary of Barrie's birth.

More than 80 events, staged entirely by local people, again between May and September, made that summer unforgettable. Especially memorable were the Thrums Dramatic Club's rendition, without professional involvement, of "Quality Street", the Purves' Puppets' animation of "Peter Pan", a Gang Show-type entertainment by over 200 local youngsters from the uniformed organisations, a costume exhibition and a procession of 21 motorised floats through the town, recalling the procession which preceded the laying of the foundation stone of the Town Hall.

That Festival climaxed with a Grand Concert in the Town Hall to mark its Centenary, consisting of a revue in prose, poetry, music, song and dance of a century of Kirrie's history. It included the re-enactment already described of Barrie's 1933 Town Band Bazaar speech, and performances by local musicians, amateur and professional, of the calibre of Joe Aitken, Angus Cameron, David Stewart and his son, Graeme, already started out on a promising professional career as Graeme Lauren, operatic tenor.

It ended with a thrilling entertainment by the talented young people who will be the future "heritors" of Kirriemuir.

The cover of the 1960 Centenary Festival Programme.

May 9th, 1985: 125th Anniversary of Barrie's Birth. Wreath laid by Mrs. Elizabeth Drainer (current Curator of Barrie's Birthplace), accompanied by (L to R) Mrs. Sandra Affleck (ACE Publicity), Miss Olga Bennell (Retired Curator), Mr. Stewart (National Trust), Sq. Ldr. 'Jock' Farquharson Urquhart (Chairman ACE), Mr. Robertson (Stonemason), Mr. W. B. Mills (Kirriemuir Herald).

APPENDIX
SIR J. M. BARRIE'S FAMILY TREE

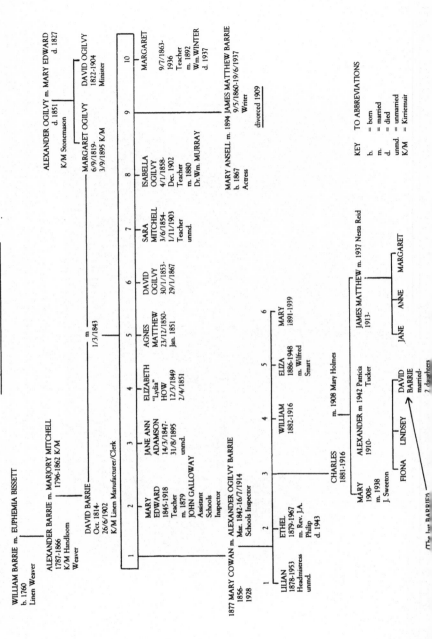

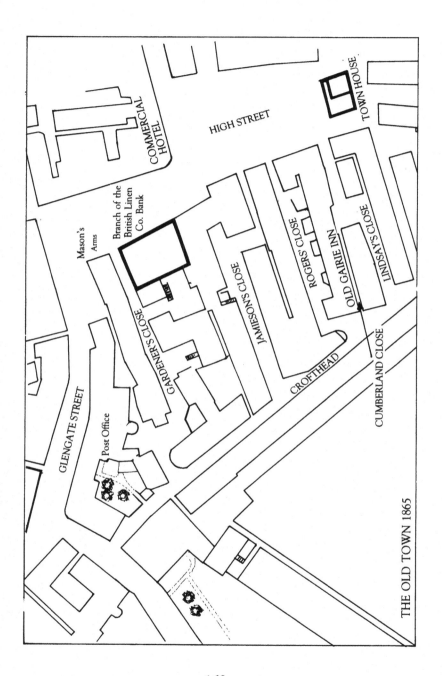

HIGH STREET

TOWN HOUSE

COMMERCIAL HOTEL

Mason's Arms

Branch of the British Linen Co. Bank

ROGERS' CLOSE

OLD GAIRIE INN

LINDSAY'S CLOSE

GARDENER'S CLOSE

JAMIESON'S CLOSE

CROFTHEAD

CUMBERLAND CLOSE

GLENGATE STREET

Post Office

THE OLD TOWN 1865

THE J.M.B. CONNECTION

LIST OF ILLUSTRATIONS
and their sources

Key to Sources

N.T.S.   Old photographs belonging to the National Trust for Scotland, plus sketch from "A Birthplace in Thrums".

A.D.L.   Old photograph collection accumulated by Angus District Libraries and Museums Department.

J.A.H.   Photographs originally published in J. A. Hammerton's "Barrie: The Story of a Genius".

D.C.T.   Photographs originally printed in "The Dundee Courier and Advertiser", copyright to D. C. Thomson Ltd.

W.B.M.   From Mr. W. B. Mills' personal collection.

St. A.   Photograph belonging to St. Andrew's Church, Kirriemuir.

A.B.   Photograph first produced in Andrew Birkin's "Barrie and the Lost Boys".

K.H.   Photograph first printed in the "Kirriemuir Herald".

D.F.   Photograph first printed in Duncan Fraser's "Land of the Ogilvys".

A.R.   Photograph first printed in Alan Reid's "Regality of Kirriemuir".

J.D.A.   Photography by my husband, J. David Affleck.

To all of these also, my sincere gratitude.

S.A.

RESEARCH SOURCES AND ACKNOWLEDGEMENTS

I am deeply indebted to all the following publications for their considerable contributions to the sum of my knowledge about Kirriemuir and Barrie.

For "FROM HAMLET TO TOWN":

George Sampson:	"From Hamlet to Town" (unpublished).
Alan Reid:	"The Regality of Kirriemuir" 1909
Angus Historic Buildings Society:	"Historic Buildings of Angus"
John F. Mills:	"Through Thrums" 1896
David Allan:	"Historical Sketches of Kirriemuir and Neighbourhood" 1865
First United Free Church, Kirriemuir:	"150th Anniversary Book 1773-1923"
Drummond & Bulloch:	"The Scottish Church 1688 - 1843"
J.H.S. Burleigh:	"A Church History of Scotland" 1960
J. Stirton:	"Thrums and its Glens" 1896

The Statistical Accounts of 1792 and 1833.

Rev. John Skinner:	"Third Statistical Account of Angus 1977"
Cheape and Sprott:	"Angus Country Life" 1980
G. F. Barbour:	"Alexander Whyte" 1923
J. M. Barrie:	"Margaret Ogilvy" 1896
J. M. Barrie:	"Auld Licht Idylls" 1888

The files of the "Kirriemuir Observer" and the "Kirriemuir Free Press"

For "THE J.M.B. CONNECTION":

Denis MacKail:	"The Story of J.M.B." 1941
Olga Bennell:	"Sir James Barrie, Bart." in "A Guide to Kirriemuir & District" 1981
National Trust for Scotland:	"A Birthplace in "Thrums"
National Trust for Scotland:	Companion Notes to Barrie's Birthplace
Andrew Birkin:	"Barrie and the Lost Boys"
Cynthia Asquith:	"Portrait of Barrie"
Janet Dunbar:	"J. M. Barrie: The Man behind the Image"
J. A. Hammerton:	"Barrieland: A Thrums Pilgrimage"
J. A. Hammerton:	"Barrie: The Story of a Genius"
Davies (publisher):	"McConnachie and J.M.B."
G. F. Barbour:	"Alexander Whyte" 1923
Mary Soames:	"Clementine Churchill"
J. M. Barrie:	"Margaret Ogilvy"

The files of the "Kirriemuir Observer" and the "Kirriemuir Free Press"

A few people deserve particular thanks:

My husband, David, for his consistent support and encouragement, as well as precious hours spent with camera and developer; our son and daughter, Graham and Gillian, for their long-suffering; Michael Visocchi for tremendous help with photographs; W.B. Mills for constant interest, information and invaluable helpfulness; my mother and Helen Main for assistance with typing; Elizabeth Drainer for her willing help with research at Barrie's Birthplace and the Angus Folk Museum, and for script checking; Mr. Ian Dale of Angus Handloom Weavers, Olga Bennell, Peter Youngson, John McRitchie and Arthur Daw for further research, manuscript reading and assessment; and my printers for all their expertise.

S.A. 1989.

168

INDEX

169

170

172

173

174

175

Lightning Source UK Ltd.
Milton Keynes UK
UKOW05f1652300617
304420UK00001B/28/P